how **HAPPY FAMILIES** *happen*

how
HAPPY FAMILIES
happen

• • • • • • ▣ • • • • • •

SIX STEPS
to
Bringing EMOTIONAL
and
SPIRITUAL Health
into Your Home

• • • • • •

Audrey Ricker, Ph.D.
with
Robert E. Calmes, Ed.D., *and* Lynn Wiese Sneyd

◧ HAZELDEN®

Hazelden
Center City, Minnesota 55012-0176

1-800-328-0094
1-651-213-4590 (Fax)
www.hazelden.org

The names and some details of the stories in this book have been
changed to protect anonymity.

ISBN-13: 978-1-59285-308-3
ISBN-10: 1-59285-308-0

10 09 08 07 06   6 5 4 3 2 1

Cover design by David Spohn
Interior design by Ann Sudmeier
Typesetting by Stanton Publication Services, Inc.

This book is dedicated
to **JOHN B. GARLAND,**
who provided invaluable support
in every kind of way
during the writing of it.

······ • ⊡ • ······

Contents

Acknowledgments

So many wonderful people contributed to this book. We extend a very special thank you to Karen Chernyaev for her intelligent, sensitive, and creative editing of the manuscript and another to our agent, Gene Brissie, for his efforts in finding the perfect publisher.

Psychotherapist and clinical director Robert Kafes, DCSW, ACSW, LCSW, made kindness, caring, and especially empathy, among other family values, not just important but interesting and exciting as well. Psychotherapist and hospice social worker Claudia Lorber, LCSW, willingly shared her knowledge of family dynamics in all stages of life, while adjunct psychotherapist Joyce Selenkow, LAC, offered invaluable expertise. We deeply appreciate your time and talents.

Finally, we want to acknowledge the Wild Oats Speedway store in Tucson for being such an ever-present refuge during the writing of this book. By providing education, caring, conversation, and such community events as weekly organic potlucks, among other forms of nurturing, this store consistently demonstrates its dedication to the spirit of the family.

chapter 1

······ ⊡ ······

The Amazing Synergy of the Six Step Plan

When it comes to creating a happy home, most of us recognize the importance of behavior, diet, and health. But these important factors are only part of the equation. Children can utter every "please" and "thank you" on cue, eat all their broccoli and brussels sprouts, and never get an ear infection, and still the underlying mood of the home may not be positive. By positive, we mean nurturing, productive, joyful, peaceful, contented, and loving. Combine all these attributes, and you have a happy home, a place where everyone is glad to be.

Sometimes people think that if everyone in a home loves one another enough, happiness will just happen. Unfortunately, that's not always true. Family members can love one another and still not get along. They may struggle to maintain pleasant relations until someone finally says or does something to tip the scales, and everyone blows up. In other homes, family members may argue day and night. Or long, cold silences may seep into every corner of a home. Sadness, too, may permeate a home for years on end. Relatives may have a hard time interacting with one another, making one another feel more like boarders than an integrated family. Then again, a home can be happy for years but turn miserable after a job loss or other catastrophic event. It's all too easy to create an unhappy home, but turning it into a happy one is not as difficult as you may think.

This book will help families turn their unhappy home into a happy one. If a home is already a pretty neat, joyful place in which to live most of the time, the following pages will offer ways to increase that happiness. Educational psychologist Dr. Robert E. Calmes has developed a method that you can use every day to make your home a more nurturing, comfortable place. For thirty years, Dr. Calmes studied thousands of families to determine what factors and characteristics contributed to their happiness. From his research, he developed a Six Step Plan. This book describes how to use this plan to turn a home into a place where people naturally congregate, a place that nurtures and renews the spirit, a place where love abounds. Of course, a happy home does not preclude the presence of strife or anger or sadness. Such conditions are inevitable in life. But a happy home is a healing home. It provides all the family members with the opportunity to transform the negative in their lives into the positive.

Before we delve into the Six Step Plan, let's explore a potpourri of happy and unhappy homes.

Our first family resides in an East Coast suburb established in the 1920s, where grand maples and oaks line the sidewalks, offering thick shade. This family of six lives in one of the many bungalows of roughly two thousand square feet. The mother and father have college degrees and full-time jobs. Their four children, three girls and a boy, are under age nine. During the school year, a college student resides in one of the upstairs bedrooms in exchange for providing child care.

The home is decorated with furniture in different styles. It was all bought secondhand, mostly at rummage sales. At the moment, a project involving a colorful array of felt pieces litters the dining-room table. The kids are making puppets for a puppet theater. A few months ago they constructed kites. Their parents spearhead these family projects, and many happy hours are spent around the table.

It's a Saturday afternoon, and the kitchen is bustling with activity. The mom is getting her kids, plus four other neighborhood children, juice boxes. She'll then pour iced tea for two other moms who stopped by to visit.

This house is frequently full of people, from family members to friends to neighbors. Even the college boarder's friends periodically come over to hang out with the family. Both parents have always been passionately interested in other people. They are compatible and have an easy relationship with each other, a relationship that extends to those around them. For many reasons, people feel welcome in this home.

Our next family consists of a mother, a father, and six children ages six to eighteen at the time of this writing. Neither parent works, because they are supported by trust funds. The family spends winters in Aspen, Colorado, where they reside in a spacious five-thousand-square-foot home near the base of a ski resort. The children have all the hottest ski gear and clothing. At night, they relax in a hot tub or watch a movie on a big-screen TV while a fire roars nearby in a giant stone fireplace. More than once a week, this family entertains an assortment of friends and relatives, be it with fondue and smorgasbords or Warren Miller ski movies. They are generous with their wealth, and all who visit feel welcome.

During the week, a hired teacher comes to the home to tutor the kids from 9:00 A.M. to 2:00 P.M., and then everyone takes off to ski the mountains. When summer arrives, the family migrates to the high Alps in Switzerland, where enough snow still covers the runs to support their skiing habits. Some of the children aspire to be Olympic skiers; others want professions completely removed from skiing. The parents are not particular. They will be happy with whatever careers their children choose. They feel grateful for the opportunity to ski as a family throughout the year and for the quality of their family life.

But you don't need six children and a stash of money to be happy. In fact, size of family doesn't matter. In a *New York Times Magazine* article titled "The Family Mobile," author Melissa Fay Greene described several large families with fifteen or more members. These families only grow happier as more children are adopted. Some of the children have disabilities. These homes are so happy, so stable, that new children eventually succumb to the happiness and encouraging, positive atmosphere no matter how severe their physical or emotional problems.

On the other hand, a family of two can exude happiness. One husband and wife we met, both actors on television and in films, made the decision not to have children because of the demands of their careers. They are content in their marriage and love for each other, yet they love children and have realized children were missing from their lives. So, when time permits, they share their home with their friends' children.

"When we have time off," the wife said with a laugh, "we just borrow some kids from friends or relatives for a week or so. We do all these things with them at home, like play board games, put on plays, and cook up fabulous meals. It's so much fun. They don't seem to mind that we limit their video games and TV to no more than an hour a day."

When it's time to say good-bye, the children, who feel welcomed and loved during their stay, clamor to return for another visit.

Single parents can have especially happy homes, as our next family shows. Jan, a single mom in New York, got custody of her three boys, now fifteen, fourteen, and twelve, when they were very small and she was in her mid-thirties. "At first I thought I could never raise these kids on my own," she said. Her ex-husband couldn't be depended on to help; he had gone to live in Spain and said he wanted no part of family life ever again. But Jan did succeed in raising the boys by herself. She's now almost fifty and very happy with her family life. She gets support for being a single parent from friends, Big Brothers Big Sisters, and membership in various organizations, such as the YMCA. She has an active social life that allows her to model dating skills, and she cheerfully learns how to do the activities her boys enjoy—such as skateboarding. "It's really fun and great exercise," Jan reported. She also expects the boys to do housekeeping and cooking chores, and they do. "They know I can't do everything," she said. And, being close in age, the boys depend on one another for friendship. "That's a big plus," Jan said. "I never have to worry about them being lonely, which is so great."

The film *Little Man Tate* illustrates another happy single-parent family. In it, Jodie Foster plays an unwed mother who is an uneducated blue-collar worker. When her son proves to be a genius, he is taken away from her to live with Jane, a gifted-child expert played by Dianne Wiest, who feels certain that she can provide a more enriched environment for the child. She has a professionally decorated home full of amenities, conveniences, and a plethora of expensive, educational toys. Alas, she lacks a life.

"What's wrong with you, Jane?" the boy yells at her one day in frustration. "Nobody ever comes over!"

He then returns to the small apartment that he shares with his mother. Seeing how happy he is to be back home, Jane realizes that children need more in life than intellectually stimulating toys. The last scene shows her in the boy's apartment, celebrating his birthday with him and his mother.

Here's a quick peek at other happy homes. In one home, both parents are busy, busy, busy—so busy, as the incredibly overscheduled dad put it, they are "too busy to chew." Yet their home is happy. Another couple we know writes books and works full time at demanding careers, has two kids, and has a consistently happy, nurturing, and exciting home. A single mother of five who works at two jobs, sometimes three, maintains a happy, loving abode for all who reside there.

So Tolstoy was wrong when he said that all happy families are alike. Happy families and happy homes differ in myriad ways, from size to gender orientation to age to financial status to physical location. Families don't necessarily need to live in a picture-perfect home, although magazines and television suggest otherwise. They convey the message that if we decorate our home using correct feng shui principles, butcher-block surfaces, and Martha Stewart pastels; keep it sparkling clean with the many products advertised; and ensure that everyone gets to various activities on time, our homes will be joyful from morning till night. But that may not be the case. We can do all of these things and, despite our best intentions, our home may remain an empty shell where no one wants to be, at least not for very long.

Look at this unhappy family, for instance. As with some of the other families, the mother and father work in professional careers outside of the house. They have six children, three boys and three girls under the age of ten. Their home is large and looks like it came straight out of *House Beautiful.* Surfaces are smooth and uncluttered. Every detail, from baseboard trim to cornice decoration, matches in some subtle way.

When outside of the house, the family appears happy. They do things like stroll shopping malls and eat in bright, family-friendly restaurants. The parents attend their kids' dance recitals and karate tournaments.

This picture of unity, however, disintegrates when they step into their home. There, the mood turns bleak. Interaction deteriorates into bickering and connections fade as everyone turns inward, toward individual projects. Most of the time the kids watch television or play video games by themselves.

Meals, when eaten together, are accompanied by whining and such expressions of distaste as "I hate green spaghetti; I want white" and children leaving the table in tears. Having long since given up on having happy meals with the kids, the parents sit silently, refilling their glasses of wine.

Only when plans are under way for an event in the house, such as a birthday party or a holiday celebration, does the mood brighten. Then, for a brief few days, family members unite to prepare for the upcoming big day. But afterward, they go back to being their usual whining, bickering, unhappy selves.

Despite all its advantages, this home is not happy. We've included many other examples of unhappy homes throughout this book.

Why such disharmony in these kinds of homes? Well, the answers vary. Some parents, for instance, never lived in a happy home as children and lack experience in creating happiness. They truly have no idea what a happy home feels like. A second reason for unhappiness is that parents have busy schedules, and while they may be proficient at work and participate in community activities, they don't put forth the effort to keep things happy and peaceful at home. Perhaps they are too tired and stressed to care. Third, many modern homes have so much space and such a multitude of televisions and media players that family members can go days without seeing or talking to each other for more than a meal or to say good-night. Loneliness may be an issue. A spouse may travel week in and week out, or a single parent may work long hours and not reserve sufficient time and energy for the children, who remain at home unattended. Other reasons for unhappiness include anxiety and fatigue.

Moreover, one family member may feel as though he or she doesn't belong, another might be the domineering sort who tries to boss everybody around, or the personalities between spouses or a parent and child may clash. Also, a family member might be suffering from chronic illness. When people are in pain or discomfort, they can behave as miserably as they feel.

Whatever the reason for a home's unhappy mood, you can take steps to make it happier. This book provides an effective, easy-to-follow formula that can improve the mood exponentially. If the mood of your home is already pleasant and welcoming, applying the formula will make it even more exciting and full of loving feelings.

The formula is simple. It involves practicing six modes of behavior that, when operating simultaneously, are synergistic. They work together to create a happy, inviting, wonderful-to-be-in home. Some of the behaviors may feel unfamiliar to you. That doesn't mean that they aren't suited for you. It merely means you need practice using them. They will be especially effective for you and will increase not only your happiness but the happiness of those around you. Using these steps can result in a happier home in a surprisingly short time—in just a few days. One thing is for sure: In the process of practicing these steps, you will find that you are more loving and, in return, more loved.

Implementing these steps is sort of like doing a craft project—it's creative and useful at the same time. Although you may have nothing tangible to hang on your wall or place on a bookshelf, you will have an ever-growing tapestry of joy, an ever-expanding wall hanging of happiness. These steps won't resolve serious problems such as drug addiction or depression, but they will make them easier to handle.

So how happy is your home? Following is a questionnaire that you can complete to get a general idea. Maybe the results will open your eyes; maybe they will corroborate what you already know. The purpose of the questionnaire is to establish a baseline reading of "home happiness" so that as you apply the Six Step Plan to your family life, you will be better able to gauge the results of the changes you have made.

Score every statement with a number between one and five, with five being the most true and one the least true.

- My home is often chaotic.
- My home is often empty.
- I'm expected to do everything in my home.
- Sometimes I would rather stay at work or anywhere else than come home.
- It seems as though I lose touch with my family when I'm at home.
- Dinners at home are complaint fests.
- My family goes out to eat fast-food meals most of the time because it's the only way we can have even halfway happy meals.
- It seems like I'm usually home by myself—everyone else in the family is out somewhere.
- My kids rarely seem happy at home.
- I make up my mind that I'm going to be nice to my family no matter what happens, but I can't stick to the plan.

Now add up your score. If it is between 36 and 50, keep reading—you really need this book.

A score between 21 and 35 indicates that you have a happy home some of the time but could make it more nurturing and peaceful.

A score between 11 and 20 means that you have the hang of creating a happy home and you are at the fine-tuning stage.

Finally, a score of 10 means you probably have a wonderful

home where everyone is happy most of the time. In that case, this book will help you see what you are doing right and encourage you to share the Six Steps with others to help them create happier homes.

······························
Defining Your Values

Clarifying family values is essential for succeeding in the Six Step Plan. Happy families are families with happy parents—and happy parents are parents who know the family is expressing those values that are most important to the parents. So, you have to know what your values are for your family if you are going to help your family achieve them. What is a value? A value is a state of being you care about. Honesty, for instance, is an ethical state of being on which you might place a lot of importance. Honesty becomes a family value when you believe it is important for each individual and the family as a unit to practice being honest.

We organize values into four categories: spiritual, intellectual/physical (we combine intellectual and physical into one value because one is necessary for the other), ethical, and emotional. Dr. Calmes says you may choose to add a fifth category—aesthetic values, or how you want you, your family members, and your home to look, at least most of the time.

To discover your family values for these categories, sit down with five sheets of paper, each labeled across the top with a value category. We had a friend do this exercise, a single mom of three who works full time as a teacher. We asked her to state her values first, and then explore the ways that she wants her family to express these values. Here are her results:

- Intellectual/physical values: I value good grades for my kids. I value intellectual curiosity. I want all my kids to at least engage with their schoolwork enough to learn. I want them to be curious all the time—lifelong learners. I value artistic expression. I want to resume my artwork and learn how to paint murals. I value physical health, which means preferring healthy food to junk food and doing more bike riding together on a regular basis, maybe Sunday mornings before church, because we enjoy it and it keeps us in shape.

- Spiritual values: I value believing in a higher spiritual power. If my kids want to be agnostics, I want them to be able to trust that there is a higher power that cares about them. I value regular church attendance because it encourages regular spiritual belief. I want my kids to continue going to our church (even if they complain about it) till they're old enough to live on their own, because regular churchgoing is what I value for me right now—I love my church and the people in it— and for them, too.

- Emotional values: I value openness and emotional expressiveness. I value accepting people for who they are. I value acceptance of people's negative emotions. I value hopefulness. I want my kids and me to be able to be open emotionally with one another but be able to control the negative emotions enough to get along. I want my kids to be able to love people for who they are, not for what they can provide—i.e., popularity, status, money.

- Ethical values: I value being honest, doing the right thing, being fair to others, being generous to others, being happy with what you have. For myself, I value being a good mother and a good role model, because those things are more important than giving them money and a good dad—both of which I am unable to do at this time.

- Aesthetic values: I value stylishness and attractiveness. I value "less is more, with no clutter." I want to look cool and keep my figure because I like looking nice. I want my children to dress modestly and like preppie kids because that is the look I like best. (Just kidding.) But I do want my two daughters to avoid using bare flesh as an accessory because it arouses boys physically. I like my home to be clean, uncluttered, and not falling apart. So there.

This exercise took our friend all of seven minutes and proved very instructive for her. Just remember to be honest when you do this exercise. Avoid thinking about your answers too much. Your list of values could be different; for instance, it could include more instructions and details. It should concentrate on positive values as much as possible instead of dwelling on what you don't value. Your list can include goals for achieving these values, if you want to add them after your "I value . . ." statements.

Once you have clarified your values, you can file the list and keep it in mind. Refer to it often as you read and use this book.

chapter 2

•••••• • ☐ • ••••••

The Six Step Approach Explained

This chapter will begin with an outline of the Six Step Plan to creating a happy home. It then will explore the synergy between the steps and how they work together like fibers in a woven fabric to generate an appealing, positive atmosphere in the home. In addition, it will address why the Six Steps are modules that can be used in any order or combination. Finally, this chapter will discuss ways in which the four characteristics that hurt a home most are rendered less destructive and even healed by the Six Step Plan.

Every step in the Calmes Six Step Plan to a happy home is really a separate process that in itself will improve the home. When combined, these processes acquire even more power to make life better in many ways. Here the Six Steps are explained, in brief:

•••••••••••••
Modeling

This is the "do-as-I-do, not-as-I-say" step. It assumes that the real message of a parent lies in her actions, not her words. Think of a favorite teacher you had. How did she act? What did he model? What behaviors did she display that meant a lot to you? Audrey's favorite teacher was Mrs. Cranmer, in third grade. She acted like an elegant lady, always perfectly dressed, coiffed, and groomed. She modeled orderliness and persistence. Her behaviors included dusting off her chair before she sat down, smiling all the time, and painting her oval nails with nail polish named Windsor Rose (Audrey knows because she asked). Mrs. Cranmer was strict but fair, and her rules were meant to facilitate learning. She modeled patience with students who couldn't keep their desks tidy (Audrey's problem) or couldn't add more than three figures (also Audrey's problem), and she accentuated students' strengths.

....
Consistency

This step means always being the same person, no matter how tired or upset or angry you might feel. You can be Mom who is angry, but not that raging monster Mom turns into when she gets mad. You can be Mom who gets worried when Dad loses his job or Johnny gets an F in algebra, but you can't be that maudlin, hysterical stranger Mom turns into every time something goes wrong. Consistency, in other words, means holding on to the self through thick and thin, on a 24/7 basis, 365 days a year. Research shows that children do best when their home life is consistent. If it is consistently positive, the children usually thrive and go on to have consistently positive lives of their own. If their home life is consistently negative, children often reject the family and find more positive lifestyles to emulate. But inconsistent home lives that are positive for a while and then destructive can make children hopelessly dependent. Hoping against hope the family will stay in a positive mode, these children tend to cling somewhat desperately to their home situation, never able to thrive on their own or to reject the family completely so they can build a life of their own.

Reinforcement

This step involves acknowledging people in your family when they demonstrate or model desired behaviors. Reinforcement is a mild and casual form of attention. It's present but not overbearing. Let's say that helping around the house, obeying curfew rules, and working diligently on homework every day during homework time are desired behaviors. These behaviors can be reinforced with conversation ("I see you're revising that paper you got a C on"), with tangible help ("Sure, I'll do the dishes if you have to study for that test"), and by modeling your willingness to do what you are supposed to be doing in life (working, housecleaning, parenting) with consistency. Reinforcement is also the attitude with which this help, acknowledgment, and modeling are conducted. The attitude should be neither wildly happy nor self-pitying, but consistently positive.

There's a fine line between reinforcement and praise. Praise is a reward to be given infrequently. Praise is best reserved for when a family member meets a big challenge, like when a child with a disability endures an entire game of wheelchair tennis or when a child holds a demanding part-time job yet manages to graduate with honors. Praise given for tasks that are not challenging tend to diminish the child's incentive to excel. Reinforcement, however, provides the child enough of an ongoing positive feeling to make him believe that the task is a good thing to do and worth his best efforts even in the hardest of conditions.

Kids whose desired behavior is reinforced learn how to feel good about their efforts most of the time. Reinforcement needs to be consistent. It means offering consistent appreciation for honest effort in the form of a smile, nod, "good job," "attaboy," or maybe an offer to lend a hand. Reinforcement can take the form of something substantial, as in an offer to pay a chunk of a hardworking student's college tuition, but most of the time it can be small, as small as a special smile— and frequent, but not so frequent that it's taken for granted or distrusted as being insincere.

Showing Rational Empathy

There is a subtle yet major difference between empathy and sympathy. Being sympathetic means feeling pity, while showing empathy means at least trying to understand why a person feels and acts as she does. That person in turn feels "known"—a state of being that, as therapists know, is extremely healing. In their book, *How to Talk So Kids Will Listen & Listen So Kids Will Talk,* authors Adele Faber and Elaine Mazlish turn empathic treatment into an art form and show how the use of empathy can be a very effective way of dealing with kids' unwanted behaviors. Audrey can vouch for the fact that nothing on earth is more of a gift than empathy to people in psychic despair. A gift of a million dollars in small bills would not be as much comfort because money cannot buy the kind of healing that empathy provides. To have empathy is to care why someone in the family is acting badly, as opposed to taking the behavior personally and getting bent out of shape.

To be effective, rational empathy needs to make sense to the person providing it. You would not say, "I know you feel like punching your sister so hard in the arm that you bruise her," for instance, because you don't believe that punching is a rational response. That kind of act is just not acceptable for any reason. But you can say with true empathy, "I understand that you get annoyed with your sister when she cleans your CDs by dunking them in the toilet," because you would get very annoyed with such an act yourself!

•••••••••••••••••••••••••••••••••
Showing Care and Concern for Animals, Plants, and Nonliving Things in the Home

The fact that Mrs. Cranmer was so fussy about her clothes that she dusted off chairs before sitting might strike some as obsessive. But to her students, it was a sign that she valued her physical self and her lovely clothes. Students were charmed by the delicate lace handkerchief with which she dusted her chairs, the snail-shaped curls in her silver hair, and the subtle daintiness of the African violet plant on her perfectly arranged desk. Her students knew somehow that caring for herself was also a way of caring for the classroom and thus, for them. Mrs. Cranmer demonstrated this caring every morning by standing near the door and greeting each student personally.

You do not have to be as perfect as Mrs. Cranmer to display caring for plants, animals, and nonliving things in ways that make your family feel good. You just have to place enough value on these objects to illustrate that they are special enough to be in your home. In our culture of planned obsolescence—with homes full of objects purchased, tossed aside, and forgotten, and with food meant to taste good but not to nourish—this step is especially important.

•••••••••••••••••••••••••••••••••
Showing Care and Concern for All the People in the Home

This step is not as obvious as it may sound. In *The Nanny Diaries,* the young nanny can handle just about everything— the added duties, unpredictable hours, having to shop for her boss's mistress, getting stuck with more than a dozen other children to care for during vacation, and other occupational burdens. The only thing she can't deal with is being made to feel invisible. "People look right through me," she once cries to her boyfriend in desperation. "It's as though I don't exist." She doesn't matter as a person to her employers and neither, most of the time, does the child she is hired to care for. As you'll see in the chapter on this step, *all* the people in a house have to matter at *all* times.

The Six Steps can be done in any order and work best when used simultaneously, like instruments in an orchestra. Let's take a family that lives by the Six Step philosophy. All the people are given loving attention, all the plants are kept watered, and the furnishings are kept polished and carefully placed. Only those animals that can be afforded are in the home—well brushed, fed, equipped, walked, and played with.

Now, see how all the steps work together in the family's life: Providing special toys, plants, and/or pets for family members is a way of showing care for the human beings in the house. Showing empathy means understanding when someone has a problem with a friend, a teacher, a homework project, a plant or pet, or an object, such as a broken toy or a style of clothing. Reinforcing means verbalizing appreciation for the way the family works and acknowledging behaviors that parents value. And modeling means displaying how family members should act toward one another, their plants, their pets, and the things they own.

....
How Problems in the Home
Are Healed by This Plan

Besides delineating the Six Steps to creating a happy home, we also define the four worst parenting traits: narcissism, neglect, playing favorites, and abusive behavior. The Six Step plan can help eliminate these traits. Here's how:

NARCISSISM

The parent who is a narcissist, or self-involved, can learn to refocus his preoccupation with himself onto his family if he practices caring about the people, plants, animals, and things in his house; practices expressing empathy to all family members; models caring behavior with consistency; and reinforces family members when they reflect behaviors that show they care about themselves, their belongings, their pets, and others in the family.

NEGLECT

Let's use the example of children who neglect their pets. Instead of complaining about this neglect, threatening to get rid of the pet, and angrily taking care of the pet themselves, parents using the Six Step plan will begin modeling good pet care. Instead of caring for the pet themselves, the parents will involve the children in their care of the pet. They will tell the child as they go about the pet-care chores how the pet enjoys and benefits from walking and bathing and playing and being fed. This modeling of pet care will need to continue consistently for about a week before the child begins to do it on her own. (The parent can expedite this process by saying something like, "I have an appointment tonight, so I can't be with you when you walk Spot and feed him.") As the parent sees the child assume more and more of the pet-care responsibilities, the parent reinforces his efforts with such words as, "You are making that dog really happy. Also healthy." When the parent finds out the child has forgotten a pet-care chore, the parent shows empathy by saying, "I know you were thinking of something else and forgot feeding (walking, playing with) Spot." Instead of scolding, the parent can then model empathy for the pet. "I know Spot really enjoys (eating, walking, playing) and must have been disappointed." The child will then understand how the dog felt and explain why she forgot—and maybe even apologize.

PLAYING FAVORITES

The parent who practices the favoring of one person over others in the family will not only become aware of this tendency when practicing the Six Step Plan but will be able to stop it. By caring for all the people in the home, not just her favorites, that parent will show empathy for everyone, which means appreciating everyone for him- or herself, reinforcing everyone's desired attitudes and behavior, and modeling this care of all people with consistency. By providing consistent attention to everyone, the parent will become more aware of every family member's uniqueness and thus become interested—genuinely interested—in every person as a special individual who possesses interesting abilities and traits.

ABUSIVE BEHAVIOR

In some cases, the Six Step Plan can get abusive parents back on track—but in cases where mental illness or a learned pattern is being repeated, therapy, medication, or intervention is necessary. Let's take the case of a famous mother who, according to her daughter's autobiography, became physically abusive to her daughter when they were alone together. Had this mom been practicing the Six Steps, she might have been able to halt the rage attacks before they started. She would have known that hitting her daughter was not modeling the kind of behavior she wanted her daughter to follow, and she would have known it was not consistent with her "nice mother" behavior in public. This mother would have been able to reinforce herself in some way for keeping a grip on her rage. She would have shown rational empathy for herself—and thus her daughter—by telling her daughter that she could feel herself going into a bad mood. Finally, she could be sure to add that the mood was not the result of anything her daughter had done. This mother could have shown care for pets, plants, and things at that moment by perhaps clearing the table or filing her nails or doing some other physical task that lets off steam. And she would have shown care for her daughter by not allowing herself to vent her rage on this child who had done nothing to deserve it.

Here's a real secret of success behind the Six Step Plan: It removes the focus from the negative acts and attitudes in the home and redirects that focus to acts and attitudes that are positive.

Another secret of the plan's success is its flexibility. Why is it flexible? Because it is nonlinear. The steps can be used at any time in any order on an as-needed basis and, as we have already said, can and should be used simultaneously. The more you practice the Six Steps, the more you will find yourself using all of them all the time.

A word about hierarchy and the Six Steps: None of the steps is more important than any other except when a particular step needs refining. If, for instance, you are inconsistent ("Mom, you were so nice yesterday. Why can't you be nice today?"), you can concentrate temporarily on the consistency step. If you really could care less about housekeeping, plants, and especially pets, you can work on Step Five (caring for all the plants, pets, and things in your house), with more effort than you use on the other steps.

Now, on to a consideration of Step One: modeling.

chapter 3

•••••• ▣ ••••••

Step One: Modeling

This chapter explains how adult behavior sets the mood of a home. It also explores how acting the way you want others to act encourages them to act like you do.

A home reflects the moods of the adults who live in it. If parents model happy, emotionally secure, controlled, and productive moods, the other people in the home are more likely to be happy, emotionally secure, under control (meaning not acting out at will whenever they feel like it), and in good moods as *they* go about pursuing their own lives. If the mood in the home is generally stable and positive, the odds are that everyone will lead productive lives filled with love and friendship.

An important purpose of this chapter is making parents realize that children pick up on almost everything they do, say, and think (yes, thinking is communicated in subtle ways). This chapter gives examples of modeling (positive and negative) and talks about characteristics of modeling. It's like a chapter on the art of acting. Acting and modeling affect the emotions of others in ways intended by the actor doing the acting or the parent doing the modeling.

Modeling is really a form of management of the home that (unlike business management) goes on all day, every day, with a few hours off for sleep. As manager of your home, you are demonstrating leadership and doing what you think you should be doing, whether you feel like doing it or not.

Modeling is being deliberately fake sometimes—"fake it till you make it," as they say in Twelve Step programs. It's projecting an in-charge, in-control, loving, and caring demeanor most of the time, whether you feel in-charge, in-control, loving, and caring or not.

Why would we urge you to pursue such an arduous, inauthentic activity as modeling? Because, to put it succinctly, children need someone to model the kind of tone and mood you want in the home. If children don't have someone modeling an appropriate tone and mood for them, their communication can degenerate into bickering or yelling or silences loaded with hostility.

Another reason why modeling is so important is that a family's style of modeling is passed down to the next generation. Here's an example of how that works:

Generation one: Rachel, who married Robert in the 1930s, ruled over her family with a combination of temper tantrums, threats of temper tantrums if she failed to get her way, and weeping episodes that were precursors of temper tantrums. Robert adored Rachel so much that he counted a good day as one in which he was able to make things go Rachel's way often enough to ward off her tantrums. The couple's children, Beth and Richard, also defined happiness as a day without Rachel's temper tantrums. Richard, being a handsome musician whom his mother, Rachel, adored, was better at achieving this goal than Beth, who, being somewhat rebellious, never did seem to please her mother and was the object of Rachel's outbursts nearly every day.

Generation two: Richard, the handsome musician, began experimenting with drugs and alcohol in college and was a substance abuser his whole adult life. Despite active membership in AA, Richard never stopped drinking. His first wife left him because of his temper tantrums while drinking; his second wife is still with him, but is a victim of chronic fatigue syndrome and sleeps about twenty hours a day on a good day, twenty-three or twenty-four hours on a day when her symptoms are severe.

Beth married a handsome, charismatic man, Rory, a Vietnam veteran who had severe temper tantrums when he was drinking but was a good husband and father when he was sober. The marriage split up many times because of Rory's behavior when he drank. Beth missed him during these episodes and seemed unable to become romantically interested in anyone else. She vowed to learn to live with the tantrums if she and Rory reconciled. As they reconciled, Rory would always promise to stop the temper tantrums and sometimes promised to stop drinking altogether.

Generation three: Beth and Rory's son, Rory Jr., decided early in his childhood that his father was an alcoholic who was "messed up" from the war and so never blamed himself for his dad's temper tantrums. He did, however, hate his mother's submission to his dad's bad treatment and her habit of walking on eggshells all the time to avoid saying anything or doing anything that might cause his dad to get mad and start drinking. He left home at an early age, went into sales work, and became a big success. At the age of twenty-five, Rory Jr. married Sue, a gorgeous woman from a prominent wealthy family who could have been, and indeed wanted to be, a model and movie star, but was pregnant at the time of her marriage and gave up her dreams so she could breastfeed and be a mom to the baby she adored. Rory Jr. and Sue had two lovely daughters within three years. When Rory Jr.'s career advanced, Sue began having temper tantrums. When he was promoted to a more challenging job in another part of the country, Sue said she was glad. But when the move turned out to be difficult—a step down in their scale of living due to the much higher cost of living and more career challenges for Rory Jr. than he'd expected—Sue's chronic anger escalated. She is now having temper tantrums on the scale of the temper tantrums that Rory Jr.'s grandmother Rachel had. She uses the temper tantrums in the same way that Rachel did, as leverage to get her way. Unlike Rory Jr., who understood early in his life that he was not to blame for his dad's temper tantrums, his daughters worry that they are helping cause the temper tantrums their mother is having. Their guilt is reinforced when their mother blames them for doing anything that upsets her in any way. The older girl, now ten, has developed compulsive habits such as trying to hit her head with the heel of her hand hundreds of times in a row and speaks with an exaggerated lisp. The younger child is becoming very quiet and learning to stay out of her mother's way.

Rory Jr. comes home every night after nine or ten hours on a job that is not going well, hoping against hope that Sue will be nice and that he can figure out a way to keep her happy. He has already given in to most of her demands, such as shutting his mother, Beth, out of their lives because Sue thinks she is low class and not a good role model for their children.

Now, Rory Jr. is thinking of quitting his job and moving back to the city where they used to live, because that's something else Sue is demanding. He tells his mother (in his infrequent phone calls to her that he keeps secret from Sue) that he can't ever leave Sue because he won't risk losing the girls, and he knows she'll keep them from him if he ever gets a divorce.

On the other side of the family, Rachel's son, Richard, had one son, Graham, by his first wife (the one who left him). Richard loves his son dearly, and Graham has always admired his father for his musical talent. Graham, a professional musician, is married to Randa, a pretty and now very obese woman he met in college. They have two children. Graham will not allow any alcohol in his house.

Throughout this marriage, however, Graham has always had a mistress on the side with whom he maintains the kind of intellectual and emotional relationship he thinks he can't have with his wife. Randa apparently knows about the mistresses, eats obsessively to dull the pain caused by this infidelity, and lives in fear that Graham will leave her for one of them. She can't bear the thought of losing him, ever. All she has going for her are the children, to whom Graham is very attached.

We want to stress that this generational saga is absolutely true, that this family actually exists. Only the names have been changed to protect anonymity. As you can see, the modeling style in this family has been passed down in various forms from one generation to the next. The message modeled by the adults in every generation of this family is that threats, demands, favoritism, temper tantrums, and other kinds of power plays are the behaviors by which a family should be run. The people in generations two and three are so accustomed to this modeling they re-create it in their own families, either as victims or tyrants. How, you ask, could this re-creation happen when it has caused such unhappiness? The answer is that people will emulate, either consciously or unconsciously, what has been modeled for them on a continual basis. Therapists watch in amazement as clients unconsciously seek mates who will treat them exactly as their parents did.

If any of the parents in this just-described family had been practicing the Six Step Plan, however, their modeling style might have changed. They would have made themselves model healthy, positive feelings, the kind they wanted for their families, whether they felt them or not. They would have been aware of the negative emotions they didn't want to model, and they would have been able to avoid inflicting those negative emotions on their families. Their positive mood modeling would have broken the cycle of controlling, destructive, negative behaviors being passed down in this family. It might have been difficult for Rachel, the matriarch of the family just described, to model positive feelings, because she might have grown up in a tantrum-prone family. But had she decided to do so anyway, her children might have been positive, happy people and would probably have had positive, happy lives that would have been passed down through succeeding generations.

Even if begun when the kids are older and accustomed to the unhealthy modeling style, positive mood modeling can break cycles. As with any change in a household, this one might take a while to be effective. But if demonstrated consistently, this change will eventually be enjoyed—and emulated—by everyone in the family. The children will begin to feel it's okay to think positively. They will begin to trust the goodness and happiness being generated. They will then create new experiences that are positive instead of reenacting negative feelings and experiences. Children who resist the change and remain negative can be helped with individual therapy and attention from their parents.

It's just not possible to rule by tantrums and other acting-out behaviors when you're trying to implement the Six Step Plan.

Here is another example of the intergenerational effect of modeling by parents who did tend to model the Six Steps, without really knowing it.

Generation one: Minnie moved from England to New Jersey in the early 1800s when she was sixteen, as a servant girl to a family with several children. In America, she met a Lenape Indian and married him. They lived off the land her husband had been given and had five children whom Minnie and her husband enjoyed and taught to fish, dig for clams, and hunt. Minnie's husband helped her learn the kind of child-rearing practices he had experienced, such as developing close relationships with the children and nurturing their skills and innate talents. Minnie modeled appreciation of every child as an individual, spending separate time with every one every day on the activity that child loved best. When he decided to stay in New Jersey instead of moving westward with his tribe, Minnie's husband changed his name to Arch Berry and became a professional fishing guide and teacher, leading tourists from New York and Philadelphia on fishing expeditions and often taking his children with him. Minnie stayed home and cleaned fish, tended the garden, shucked clams, made clam pies and fritters, and helped every child learn all the household tasks.

Generation two: Minnie and Arch's children grew up and married and entered professions. They each had several children and loved every child as though every child were an only child, appreciated and adored. One daughter, Polly Berry, gave birth to eight sons. Every son was a wonder to her and her husband, who was also descended from the Lenape. All her boys survived diphtheria because they all nursed one another through the worst of it, staying up nights to extract from siblings' throats the thick phlegm that is fatal to diphtheria victims unless manually removed. The boys all married and went into different careers, including newspaper publisher, military officer, and building contractor. They built large Victorian-style homes on grassy lawns, sent some of their children to normal schools (teacher-training institutes) and colleges, and helped those who wanted to be fishermen buy their first fishing boats.

Generation three: These children married and had children and settled near and far but always came around for the family reunions in summer, which were held on the New

Jersey shore. Dozens of happy families could be seen at these events, with their wicker picnic baskets and beach umbrellas and men fishing in the sea and women helping toddlers wade in the foamy waves.

The Six Steps modeled by the parents in this family include consistency, empathy, caring for people and things, and probably a lot of reinforcement, considering all the happy marriages (at least twenty-three by the third generation) and productive children produced.

If you get the hang of successful modeling, the kind that incorporates the Six Steps, you will begin to find it a pleasure. You'll feel needed, loving, loved, and in charge. You'll soon find your kids imitating you in many ways. That's always greatly satisfying, as any good role model can tell you.

Here is one of our favorite examples of positive modeling in a difficult situation. Marcy, a young mother of two girls who lived in New York City, had been spending the summer visiting her parents in Maryland. The night she and her daughters arrived back in New York, they found her husband hosting a big party full of people Marcy didn't know. The apartment was a wreck, with dishes and overflowing ashtrays everywhere along with a haze of gray smoke and the smell of cigarettes and beer. Instead of blowing up, Marcy greeted her husband warmly, behaved graciously to the few guests she was introduced to, put the girls to bed, and then began cleaning up. When asked later how she could be so calm, Marcy replied that behaving graciously gave her a sense of security in this difficult situation. Marcy was modeling caring for her home and daughters and also consistency; she'd always been a loving mom, and she wasn't about to let her husband's inconsideration interfere with that role. The marriage, which had been shaky for almost a year, broke up soon afterward. Marcy is now remarried to a man who loves and respects her and her girls in a way her first husband did not.

How do you decide what behavior and attitudes to model in your home? If you don't want to use your own parents, pick a role model for yourself. You can choose from two basic categories: the accessible role model, such as the "Princess Diana type," or the inaccessible role model, such as the "Queen Elizabeth type." The accessible role model, need we add, tends to have a happier home and family. That's because inaccessible role models can make others feel bad about themselves—not acceptable, not wanted.

A documentary of Diana early in her marriage to Prince Charles shows her approaching the Queen Mother, who was walking her many dogs in the palace yard. Diana's look of open affection and happiness to see her mother-in-law is not reciprocated. The queen models inaccessibility by raising her chin and peering down at her daughter-in-law in an imperious way that communicated who was in power in this relationship. Diana's warm "hello" and attempts to converse are met with a cold "hmmm" that cuts off all conversation like a knife. You can see Diana's face fall as she realizes that her presence is not welcome. Finally, after giving an embarrassed and sad smile, Diana turns and leaves. The queen continues interacting happily with her dogs, obviously enjoying them in a way she cannot allow herself to do with her new daughter-in-law.

Which is not to say Queen Elizabeth has always been as inaccessible as this little scene made her look. As a young girl during the war, she was shown interacting with the people of England and her parents and sister in a way that was just as warmly spontaneous as Diana's. Her training in the art of being a queen may have suppressed that spontaneity. As an adult in her twenties, she was filmed for Movietone News arriving at a train station after being abroad for several weeks, greeting her mother and son, Charles, who was then just a little boy. Her mother got a brief embrace and little Charles got only a perfunctory smile and brief touch on his hair. Her role model as inaccessible mother had clearly begun.

A combination of the two styles, accessible and inaccessible, probably works best. June Cleaver, the mom in *Leave It to Beaver,* was clearly an accessible role model but with limits, as was Margaret, the mom in *Father Knows Best.* Both managed to communicate that accessibility while maintaining that l950s-style perfect image for their families at all times. Yes, they always wore shirtwaist dresses and pearls and high heels, even when cleaning the house. Yes, housecleaning time was sacred. But they were always happy to focus on any family member who needed their undivided attention and love.

Today, parents are realizing they can project any image they want, as long as they are comfortable with it. But certain characteristics of healthy and unhealthy role models are worth naming.

Traits of a healthy role model include the following:

- Dependable and reliable. Someone who keeps her word, who does what she says she will do.
- Cheerful. He sees life through a positive perspective.
- Fairly competent. If she doesn't know how to do something, such as tile a floor, she tries to learn.

Traits of an unhealthy role model include the following:

- Self-indulgent. She's willing to spend money on herself that should, for instance, go for groceries or school lunches.
- Actively addicted to something. Alcohol, prescription drugs, shopping, sex, or some other obsession means more to him than the children.
- Volatile. Someone in the family is always setting her off.
- Lazy. He is too lazy to make sure that the children are

cared for, the house is kept up, the pets fed, the plants watered, and other chores are done.

Being a good role model doesn't mean you can't make mistakes. The truly healthy role model is able to admit and take responsibility when she makes mistakes. If, for example, she puts off defrosting the refrigerator because she hates that job and one day finds all the food on the bottom shelf spoiled, she can acknowledge her part in the problem. If he shows up in sweats for a child's school presentation because he didn't allow enough time to dress properly—and knows his child is embarrassed—he can tell the child he's sorry for embarrassing him. He can apologize for not planning his time more carefully because he knows how awful the child must feel.

The unhealthy role model keeps making the same mistakes and blames others for them. For instance, she might say, "If your father hadn't made me clean out the garage today, I would have had time to get dressed!" The unhealthy role model might also deny that his mistakes are mistakes: "I have my own style, and it suits me fine." Or he makes excuses for his mistakes: "I don't have time to worry about how I look. I have better things to do." And unhealthy role models refuse to acknowledge the ways in which their mistakes impact others in the family: "I don't care if the way I look embarrasses you! I'm not like those other superficial moms who spend all their time on their looks, so you'd better get used to it." Or, they use their mistakes as a threat: "I said I wanted a no-defrost fridge, and now I better get one."

It's not a good idea to judge healthy or unhealthy role models as saints or sinners. Unhealthy role models could be suffering from a mental illness or going through a difficult transition, while parents who display healthy role modeling in public could be unhealthy role models in the privacy of their own homes.

A wonderful middle school teacher we know suddenly developed poor role-modeling traits (lashing out, not grading papers, eating sweets throughout the school day) and was forced to quit her job. Nobody cared that the cause of her poor role modeling was a bitter divorce that came upon her suddenly and unexpectedly; the parents of her students just said she'd become a bad teacher and should be replaced as soon as possible. Parents guilty of sexual abuse often appear to be healthy role models *par excellence*—the more vicious the abuse, the more positive their role modeling becomes to outsiders.

Don't get the impression that a healthy role model cannot be her own special self. She certainly can and should be. The healthy role model models the Six Steps in her own individual way. She has quirks that make her unique, and she allows other family members their quirks. She has relapses from time to time that she acknowledges and apologizes for. She models self-fulfillment in pursuing a career, education, or other personal goals.

The healthy role model might model curiosity of the intellectual sort. Books, field trips, lectures, and workshops are a part of his family's everyday life. If, for instance, someone in the family wants to know if it's possible to drive a car to Europe, everyone starts researching ferry service across the Bering Strait, the roads leading through Siberia south to Europe, and planning a hypothetical road trip to Europe that might actually take place someday.

How you can use the ideas in this chapter:

1. When you begin modeling, run through the other steps in your mind—consistency; reinforcement; showing empathy; caring for plants, animals, and possessions; and caring for people. They will then be installed into your psyche like a computer program,

and you'll start modeling them automatically in a million different ways.

2. Avoid confusing your modeling with expression of your power. When, for instance, you feel like yelling at your children to pick up their toys in five minutes, stop. Take a deep breath. Remember that the yelling is a power trip, and power trips are not what you want to model. Announce that it is cleanup time, begin cleaning up yourself, and set an egg timer if this will help, saying that the job needs to be done when the timer bell rings.

3. When you find yourself belittling, putting down, denigrating, or in any other way making anyone feel bad, stop. Apologize. If you can, put someone else in charge of your family and meditate. Or exercise. Or write in your journal. Or let yourself cry for several minutes to unleash the pent-up emotions you were taking out on your family.

4. When in doubt, smile. Fake a smile until you actually feel like smiling.

5. When all else fails, allow yourself to be charmed. Someone in your family has some trait or characteristic—maybe a lopsided grin or untamed cowlick—that can charm you. Soon you'll find many traits in all family members to be absolutely irresistible.

We hope you take away the following from this chapter: Modeling is not power tripping. It's acting admirably when the going gets rough.

No, it's not always easy to be a role model. Modeling is harder at some times than others, such as when you come home from work to bickering children, when your kids come home spoiled and indulged after visiting their noncustodial parent and that parent's new partner, or when friends are visiting and your children are acting rude. But doing your best to role-model, especially in the difficult moments, will pay off now and in the future, when your children are being wonderful models with your grandchildren.

•••••• ▣ ••••••

Step Two: Consistency

Consistency creates calmness; inconsistency creates chaos. Here, the reader will learn what constitutes consistent behavior and why inconsistency can spawn frustration, tension, and even hostility.

Consistency is the structure that contains the happy home. It is also the frame that outside forces push against but can't break.

Consider the case of the Martin family. The Martins live in Florida. They have four children—eight, ten, twelve, and fifteen—all of whom are busy and happy. Mr. Martin works in construction. Mrs. Martin is a certified nursing assistant who is employed at a nursing home.

A year ago, Caleb, a nephew, came to stay with them because his parents were hurt in a car accident. Caleb was eleven years old at the time.

Caleb was loud and strident and tried all kinds of behaviors when he first arrived. He insisted, in a demanding voice, that he be allowed to stay up and watch TV as late as he wanted. The answer was "No." He demanded that he be able to talk on his cell phone during dinner. The answer was "No." He yelled that he should not have to get up for breakfast with the family on weekends. The answer was "Yes, you have to."

••••••

He really yelled when he demanded to be allowed to listen to music on his CD player at all times in the home. The answer was "No." He demanded the Martins buy him his special triple-caffeine, triple-sugar soda. The answer was "No."

Eventually, Caleb gave up his demanding, yelling, and raging because he realized these behaviors weren't working. He saw that he was not going to be able to turn this home into his home, a place where he ruled the roost and got his way most of the time. He became a more respectful boy, doing well in school and participating in sports, which he had never done before. He began talking to other people, telling Mrs. Martin how sad he felt about his parents' accident and telling Mr. Martin how much he missed his dad. He began helping to make pancakes on Sunday mornings, taking a real interest in the way the dropped dough formed on the griddle. He found out what the Martin children thought about things and told them what he thought. And he participated in sports and clubs and made some friends at school. These friends also became friends of the Martin family and frequently stayed over for dinner.

The success of the Martins in holding off Caleb's assault on their rules and principles was the result of the behaviors they modeled and their carrying out of the other steps as well. But this success was due in very large part to their consistency. The Martins were consistent in saying "No." They did not, unlike Caleb's parents, bend, break, or in other ways weaken against the force of his will. They did not compromise, as his parents always had, by saying, "Just this once" or "Okay, you can listen to the music but you have to keep it turned down." Their strict use of consistency was softened with the use of other steps, such as reinforcement, as in "That polite tone of voice is just right, Caleb," and with rational empathy—"We know it can't be easy, having to live in a new family where you have to learn all new rules." But they remained consistent in their insistence that Caleb follow their family's rules. That's because the Martins know the value of consistency.

The acts that create consistency are often mechanical, a matter of putting one foot ahead of another. As Woody Allen once said, a lot of life is "just showing up." Consistency is in the doing, not in the results.

Consistency is not, for instance, waking up to a clean kitchen every morning; it's doing the dishes, wiping down the counters, and taking out the trash every night. Consistency is not having attractive children who seldom get colds; it's shopping for healthy foods and making sure the children eat nutritious snacks and get some exercise every day.

Parents who behave with consistency no matter what are able to endure divorce, suffer financial setbacks, be separated by war, and go through other crises without causing their children any additional emotional harm. Here are three cases that show the value of consistency in families:

The Reed family has two daughters, ages twelve and ten. Rob Reed is an account executive for an ad agency, and Edith Reed is an aspiring model and actress. As a way of controlling her weight for her career, Edith began taking Ritalin. She got her doctor to prescribe this drug—and told her husband she needed this drug—on the pretext that she had attention deficit disorder. At first, the Ritalin did render Edith more organized, efficient, and energetic, all of which met approval from Rob and her children. But after a few years, Edith developed a tolerance for the drug and got her dosage increased. Her personality underwent a change; she found she was no longer interested in being a mother (she had been a devoted mom when the girls were young, breastfeeding them both for almost two years, staging spectacular birthday parties, and decorating their rooms like Disney movie sets). Now, Edith would take off for auditions on a moment's notice and be gone for hours and hours without saying where she was. Or she would be gone for days and weeks at a time if she got an acting job out of town.

Rob understood that Edith was becoming inconsistent in her mothering and so made sure the girls got the maternal care they needed from an au pair from France. He began going to a therapist when Edith refused to pursue marriage counseling, so that he could better handle his stress and panic and deal with his strong fear of divorce, which he was beginning to think might be necessary. Finally, when Edith began taking methamphetamine she got from street dealers who were always calling her at home and showing up on the doorstep saying she owed them money, Rob saw he had to take action. He was able to place Edith in a rehabilitation program where she was detoxified but refused therapy.

Rob is now in Al-Anon, a Twelve Step support group for family and friends of addicts, on the advice of his therapist. Edith has been through rehabilitation but is not yet in recovery. She says she does not have time for the activities of recovering because she is too busy working with her agent to secure acting jobs in independent films. She's moving to Canada soon, where many independent films are made.

The girls are coming to terms with the fact that their mother stopped wanting to be in their lives. The consistency of parenting they received from their father and the au pair has enabled them to survive their mother's inconsistent parenting with relative ease and grace.

Judith and Kurt and their four children, ages four to eleven, are survivors of a double job loss in North Carolina, necessitating a major change in lifestyle. Kurt was a software engineer before his company outsourced his job, and Judith was a designer of children's clothes for a regional chain of upscale boutiques until loss of manufacturing businesses in their area caused the chain to go bankrupt. Judith and Kurt's combined income used to be $180,000, which paid the mortgage on their $400,000 home, the tuition for the children's private school, live-in child care, ski trips, and summer vacations on the Outer Banks islands.

Judith and Kurt now earn about $20,000 a year from food stamps and unemployment insurance. The latter source of income is temporary. They lost their home to foreclosure when they were unable to sell it and had to move to an apartment in a less upscale neighborhood.

The neighborhood they moved to was like a foreign country to Judith, Kurt, and their children—full of immigrants, worn-down schools, boarded-up stores, busy pawn shops, and people walking the streets inebriated or high on drugs. Their apartment has roaches, bad smells, and burn marks on the walls. But it was the only apartment they could find with three bedrooms that was under $500 a month, the maximum they could pay for rent. The tenants nearby get in fights that keep the family awake at night.

How are Judith and Kurt coping with this catastrophic change in their lives? With the same consistency they showed when they had money. They are using their new free time to take their children to the nearest library for story hours and reading times, to scour thrift shops for paintings to hide the burn marks on the walls, to participate in a food co-op so they can get fresh produce cheaply in order to prepare wholesome meals with their children's help, and to join a neighborhood center where the children can play with neighborhood kids while Judith and Kurt teach English classes. The children began picking up Spanish the first week they attended the play groups and are learning some Vietnamese, too. Judith and Kurt are enjoying their new line of work so much that they are considering getting credentialed so they can teach art and science, respectively, in local middle and high schools. Or, they might start a charter school that concentrates on teaching math and design. And they bought earplugs to make sleeping at night easier and have been inviting some of their neighbors to dinner just so the yelling will not seem so strange and anonymous to the kids.

The biggest problem Kurt and Judith face in their new life is the abundance of drugs and drug dealers. They have had to make their children aware of illegal drug dealing, prostitution, and theft because they know the children might see people in these professions every day and need to know how to avoid them.

What consistencies are Judith and Kurt showing? Consistent behavior in the face of change. They are consistent in their behaviors that take advantage of resources in their immediate environment and that make that environment as growth producing and positive as possible. It's not that they decided to make the best of a bad situation. It's that their consistent behaviors provided the structure they needed to make the best of a bad situation.

A third example of the value of consistency involves Alyssa, a single mom in her thirties, and her son, Kevin, thirteen. Alyssa was a successful entrepreneur who sold the jewelry she created at craft fairs and boutiques until an addiction to prescription painkillers caused her to lose everything. She was arrested for selling OxyContin to support her addiction, and her son was put in foster homes. During her year and a half as a resident in a halfway house, Alyssa had to learn and practice consistent behavior. She realized that her life had been very inconsistent up to then, with drug-fueled spurts of creativity lasting several days, drug-fueled marketing efforts, and drug-induced periods of sleeping for several days at a time, all the while allowing Kevin to fend for himself and to get himself to school if he wanted to go. He lived on Pepsi, french fries, and Life cereal—his favorite foods—and dressed in clothes chosen from a pile of unironed, often unwashed clothes in his closet and bureau drawers.

When criticized for her child-rearing methods, Alyssa would retort that Kevin was doing fine, was a free spirit who adored her more than most kids loved their mothers, and was considerably more self-sufficient than most kids ever had the chance to be.

At the halfway house, however, Alyssa learned from Kevin's counselor that her son hated his life and that he always worried about her and felt ashamed of the way he looked at school. He had also begun smoking marijuana with kids he wanted to be friends with—kids who were grooming him for a life in drugs, shoplifting, and prostitution for the money he needed to buy the drugs he wanted.

When Alyssa graduated from the halfway house, she secured a job in social services that paid her enough to rent an apartment in a better part of town and get Kevin into a well-supervised after-school program. She ensured that Kevin went to bed at 9:00 every night, that their time together was spent in constructive activities such as preparing meals (Kevin has a strong interest in food preparation) and riding bikes, not just watching TV together or playing video games. Kevin has lately shown sufficient talent for basketball to land him a scholarship to a private basketball league, which means Alyssa now spends most weekends washing his uniforms, driving him to practice, and watching his games. She enjoys these activities because she enjoys basketball, but mostly because she loves watching Kevin play.

These behaviors show consistency of the kind that tends to make families happy. Alyssa is also consistent at dealing with unwanted behavior from Kevin, such as his tendency to make obscene gestures when angry, which he picked up in the foster homes he lived in while his mom was in rehab. She tells him these behaviors are not acceptable, gives rational reasons why, and, if the behaviors persist, enforces consequences such as canceling plans to have his friends over or go to a movie. Alyssa has a hard time at family reunions, where all the cousins have so much more financial support and material objects than Kevin does. He feels bad about his life at these times, and Alyssa feels bad for him. But she considers the family connections so important she'll keep going to the reunions every year. Meanwhile, she uses self-talk and sometimes the help of a counselor at the treatment facility to remind herself that she's providing Kevin a life that's consistently nurturing and productive, which is a lot more than a lot of parents ever provide for their kids.

Are parents becoming more inconsistent? The following study suggests that this might be the case.

In 1999 some professors in the College of Education at the University of Arizona began to suspect that the students whom teachers were dealing with did not possess the same behaviors and attitudes as students who had been in their classes ten or even five years before. To find out whether these suspicions were valid, these professors designed and implemented a study that involved graduate students interviewing forty-six teachers in seven states. While limited, this study did yield some findings that indicate inconsistencies in parental behavior that can affect a teacher's ability to teach and a student's ability to learn.

This study was what is known as a qualitative study, meaning the data were categorized by themes rather than by statistical analyses. The teachers were interviewed over dinner in groups of not more than six. Independent note takers recorded responses made by the teachers. The researchers believed that the informal restaurant setting would make the teachers feel more comfortable about expressing their opinions.

In discussing differences they had seen in their students, the teachers also spoke of differences they were seeing in parental behavior. Many of these parental behaviors involved inconsistency. Here are some examples:

More and more, the teachers said, parents want their children to be physically fit but seem to do little to curb the amount of time their children spend being inactive. For instance, teachers in a high-socioeconomic-level private elementary school got the impression that while most of the moms were slender and fit, many of the students were overweight. Teachers in most of the schools agreed that from conversations they have with their students, they learn that parents appear to be allowing their kids to spend hours every day watching television or playing video games. In a high-socioeconomic-level high school for honor students, however, the school took responsibility for making sure students got enough exercise by requiring students to spend at least two hours every day in an aerobic sport such as swimming or track and field in order to stay enrolled in the school.

Another example of parental inconsistency reported by teachers participating in this study was that more and more parents are willing to keep children out of school despite their desire to have the children get good grades. Though these parents would declare their commitment to their children's education at parents' nights and by signing official-looking contracts for the teachers, they would keep children out of school for family vacations, to baby-sit younger siblings, while moving, and for other reasons, often for days at a time. Most of the teachers in the study agreed that prioritizing family events over school attendance was new—most parents ten years ago would not have thought of taking their children out of school for anything but a death in the family or an illness.

In addition, many parents complain that their children

have too much homework, yet they insist that their children get good grades in school. These parents, instead of encouraging their children to study hard at home, want all work to be done during school hours, and they let their children know that that's how they feel as well.

In discussing these inconsistent behaviors, the teachers did not blame the parents. They attributed these behaviors to the culture. They agreed that the culture in America seems to be changing in ways they don't really understand. They hope that both in-service (working) and preservice (student) teachers get more training in dealing with parental behaviors so they are better prepared to handle the inconsistencies in parents' behaviors when they need to do so.

A recent *Psychology Today* article entitled "A Nation of Wimps" tends to support the parental inconsistencies found in the teachers' study.* Author Hara Estroff Marano says that while parents today want their children to be successful, they create a no-fail, micromanaged life for their kids that renders many unable to cope emotionally with the sudden independence and challenges of college life. "Psychological distress" in the form of anxiety and depression "is [now] rampant on college campuses," Marano says. More students than ever act out this distress with binge drinking, "cutting," and other self-destructive behaviors.

Yes, college administrators are worried, Marano adds. She then quotes Steven Hyman, provost of Harvard University and former director of the National Institute of Mental Health, as saying that many students' mental states are now so precarious that "it is interfering with the core mission of the university."

---

* Hara Estroff Marano, "A Nation of Wimps," *Psychology Today* 79 (November/December 2004): 58.

A recent *60 Minutes* segment on the "Echo Boomers," the children of the baby boomers, showed they are the most watched-over, fussed-over, micro-nurtured generation ever seen in America, treated "like Baccarat crystal," as one psychologist on the show put it. As a result, they are attractive and confident and positive and—as another psychologist on the show said—used to being successful at getting what they want. Because of this upbringing, that psychologist fears these kids are in for a rude awakening on their first real jobs—where they are not likely to be given most things they want.

Conditions Causing Inconsistency

There are some conditions that are inherently inconsistent. The two we'll examine here are addiction and codependence.

ADDICTION

Most parents who abuse alcohol or other drugs are inconsistent. Sometimes abusive, uncaring, or explosively angry when high, these parents can be the most caring, kind, loving, and supportive of parents when sober. Family members believe that if they just try hard enough, they can stave off the next drunk or high indefinitely. They study hard, clean the house to perfection, look terrific, and act cheerful all the time. These efforts are escalated when the next binge occurs—mainly because the efforts are like lifesavers and are all the family members have to cling to during these difficult times. They can only think about doing better or trying harder at everything because that's the only way they know of to maybe (just maybe) keep their parents from getting too upset.

We know of only one way to provide such family members with consistency in their lives—by participating in Twelve Step groups like Al-Anon. These groups provide members with the framework and model for consistency they have always needed so much from their parents. Members who are able to accept this consistency from these groups are able to stop longing so desperately for their parents to change.

CODEPENDENCY

Codependent parents are also inconsistent. They can be well-functioning, consistent, caring, empathic parents to their children—until they go into their disease of codependency. Then, the entire family can be sold down the river in a heart-beat for the person on whom they are codependent. Often, that person is someone with an addiction of some kind who is not in recovery of any kind.

Take the case of Nell, a mom of four, whose husband is a compulsive gambler. This man is fine, a devoted father, husband, and school superintendent—if he stays away from the casinos. By staying away, we mean not even going to the same side of town as the casinos. If he even points his car in that direction, he is likely to go into his disease and disappear into the casino for days at a time, stopping only when he has exhausted his current financial resources and is too tired to stay awake. That's when Nell goes into action, assessing the financial loss, refinancing the house if necessary, and making up some kind of amnesia or abduction or seizure story for the school board. If necessary, she puts the house up for sale, taking the children out of school and relocating in an apartment in another part of town until her husband's contract can be bought out by the school board and he can find another superintendent job in another city or town. The children's lives are uprooted every year and a half or so, but that's the cross they have to bear. Nell believes she's a terrific wife and mother for picking up the pieces so efficiently. She justifies his gambling to herself and her children as a stress reliever he pursues when the pressures of being a school superintendent build up too high. The truth is, Nell is codependent. She structures her life—and thus the lives of her children—around her husband's addiction to gambling. The children's needs for a stable life, friends, and time to build connections in school are ignored because of their father's addiction and their mother's codependency.

When Inconsistencies Are Positive

Inconsistent behavior can, if implemented in the right way at the right time, be a marvelously spontaneous reward for working hard and following rules. In other words, the parent who is consistent all of the time can make the rare inconsistent act seem like a real treat for the family.

Joy Ann, a single parent of three, was the model of consistency all year. She worked hard at her advertising job and saw to it the children did well in school, helped with the housework, and had part-time jobs to pay for the extras that Joy Ann's salary did not cover. But every summer, Joy Ann would be happily inconsistent. She would come up with wonderful local vacation ideas that were considered and voted on by her children and then pursued by the whole family for two glorious weeks. One year they all went to a nearby dude ranch; another year, they stayed home for a week and visited a different local site of interest each day and ate at a different restaurant each night. But most years they went to a different glamorous hotel in their city and spent two weeks enjoying all the amenities the hotel had to offer. The one rule was that they could not go home for any reason. If they forgot something, they bought it at the hotel.

Notice the hidden consistencies in Joy Ann's vacation inconsistency: The vacations were always held in her hometown, which meant savings on airfare and taxis. They live in southern Arizona, where hotels and restaurants have cheaper summer rates, so the luxury and pampering were affordable. Joy Ann's children are now grown, but they love reliving memories of those vacations when they come home to visit Mom.

....
What's Hardest about Being Consistent in the Home?

When we asked parents what they found to be most difficult about being a consistent parent, the answer was almost always, "Not giving in."

We wondered about people who have been successful in demanding, competitive careers. Were they given in to as children? Or were their parents consistent in not giving in to them? To find out, we interviewed parents of children who are successful enough to be famous.

Odie Elliott is the mother of Sean Elliott, star of the University of Arizona basketball team when it went to the Final Four in 1984. He has since played for the San Antonio Spurs and been a national television sports commentator.

Mrs. Elliott said she had to be consistent, or firm, in her parenting because she was a single mom with little money. Perhaps the greatest challenge to her consistency occurred when Sean was being recruited by the NBA. The recruiters pressured her in many ways to allow Sean to skip his senior year at the University of Arizona and to go right into professional basketball. The money offered was outrageous. But Mrs. Elliott had always been consistent about the value of a college education, and she was not about to change. She held fast, and Sean got his last year of college under his belt.

Another mother of a famous person has a theory about giving in to kids. Muriel Shandling, mother of Garry Shandling, comedian and star of the classic cable comedy *It's Garry*

Shandling's Show, believes parents give in to kids because they feel guilty that they are not giving them quality time. In her family, she said, every day they turned the TV off for a time and the family would talk, laugh, and interact.

Mrs. Shandling said this consistent insistence on daily family time was also important because it was what held her family together during difficult years when her oldest son was dying of leukemia, Garry was trying to launch his career in show business, and a Japanese exchange student living with them was struggling to learn the American culture and language.

When Consistency Is Not Beneficial

It's important for you to understand why you are being consistent. What's the goal behind your consistency? If you don't know, you might be acting in a way best described as bullheaded or stubborn. Take the case of the Martins' consistent refusal to let Caleb use his cell phone at dinner. Their goal was having all the children in their household participate in conversation at dinner, even Caleb. They knew that if they gave in even a few times and let him use his cell phone at dinner, he would give up trying to participate. They would have given up trying to stop him from using his cell phone. Before long, their kids would be wanting to use cell phones. Most kids are naturals at pushing further and further until they get what they want. The Martins knew why they needed to be consistent on that issue.

But if a child has a really good reason for getting you to change your mind, he should be allowed to make his case to you—and you should listen carefully and take the issue under advisement. If you still decide not to change your mind, at least you will have appeared to be somewhat flexible. You'll learn more about this flexibility in the chapter on rational empathy.

Next, you'll be learning about reinforcement. Consistency is always easier for a parent to achieve and maintain if she uses carefully applied reinforcement. Ways of accomplishing that step are found in the next chapter, "Step Three: Reinforcement."

chapter 5

•••••• • ▣ • ••••••

Step Three: Reinforcement

Reinforcement does not mean nagging but recognizing desired behavior. This chapter will tell you how to recognize and reward such behavior with sincerity, rather than with hollow praise that a child is likely to take for granted.

Suppose you want your children to value healthy food. You model your love of healthy food by buying, preparing, and serving only fresh fruits and vegetables, whole grains, and unprocessed meats and fish and no longer allow processed, sugared, vitamin-fortified, and artificially colored food in your home. You are consistent in modeling the value you place on healthy foods by serving these foods for snacks and entrées and side dishes and salads every day, not just on weekends or when you're in the mood.

Now, thanks to your consistent modeling of your love of healthy food, your children are becoming foodies—helping you shop for and prepare meals, coming up with their own recipes, and choosing restaurants that serve only nutritious fare.

You reinforce these behaviors by commenting on them. "That brown rice risotto you made tonight is delicious." "That peanut butter you put in the grocery basket has no trans fats in it, so I'm happy you want it."

Reinforcement means having a guidance system, or, if you will, a rudder, in place that automatically lets family members know when they're behaving in ways that are on track. The best way to reinforce desired behavior is through positive interaction with the person exhibiting the desired behavior. Here's an example:

Carla, age three, was an untidy child who seldom put anything back and by the end of the day managed to scatter clothes and toys and books throughout the house. Carla's mom was almost relieved when she had to go to work full time because her life with Carla had become a nearly constant battle of wills.

Lee, the full-time babysitter, knew what to do from the beginning. First, she modeled tidiness by putting things away on a consistent basis, always telling Carla what she was doing. "We put away the Barbies in their cubbies before we take out the Teletubbies, just like this." Soon, Carla was happily tidying up along with Lee.

Every time Carla put anything away before playing with something else, Lee reinforced this desired behavior by talking about it. "Do you think we need another box for Po and Dipsy?" she would ask when Carla put a Teletubby away. "Or should the Teletubbies all be together in their own big box?" Lee would continue in a conversational, interested tone.

Children love having things discussed with them on a consistent basis, as teachers and good caregivers know well. They like it better, actually, than being thanked, praised, and rewarded.

Here's another example: Chloe is a writer of romantic fiction who has a four-year-old son, Zack. Zack used to hang on to her all day long until she began using the words *resourceful* and *self-sufficient*. When Zack would begin whining for attention, Chloe would say, "I'm being resourceful and self-sufficient, and it's time for you to be resourceful and self-sufficient." Every time Zack played with something on his own, Chloe would stop what she was doing from time to time and discuss what he was doing in a conversational way that reinforced his behavior. "Oh, I see you're rearranging the trees in your electric train town. That's very resourceful," or, "Are you doing the Reader Rabbit video by yourself? That's so self-sufficient of you." Then she would resume her work.

Both Zack and Carla understood from these interactions that what they had chosen to do was right and good and should be continued.

Had these children in the foregoing examples been praised or rewarded for what they were doing, they would undoubtedly have developed what most overpraised and overrewarded children develop—a need to be praised and rewarded and feelings of emptiness at those times when they are not being praised or rewarded.

Sometimes, parents need to reinforce the bad side of behaviors or things the child wants. We call this notion negative reinforcement.

Negative reinforcement is a bit tricky to understand. Negative reinforcement isn't about telling the child that something she did is bad or wrong. It's about reinforcing the negative effect of whatever that "something" is, in a kind and understanding way. Here are some examples of negative reinforcement:

Rather than saying, "Going to that party at Ken's house is not okay," you can say, "It's not that I don't trust Ken or you or Ken's parents. It's that I know Ken's parents believe that kids don't need adults around when they party. That belief opens the door to far too many unwanted possibilities."

Rather than saying, "Tina, that T-shirt you remodeled makes you look indecent! There are just a few scraps of fabric left and they barely cover your chest!" you could say, "That outfit shows a lot of your body, Tina. That's not a good idea because the sight of a girl's exposed body can have unwanted effects on boys' sexual instincts. Trust me, boys' sexual instincts are very strong in their teenage years."

In both these examples, the child needed to be informed that the outfit and unchaperoned parties were negative without being led to believe that he or she was negative.

Sometimes, the child can figure out the negative ramifications of certain behaviors for herself but still needs to know what her parents' attitude is on the subject. The following case history from a social worker named Alice provides a rather dramatic example:

Alice is working with Lulu, an eighteen-year-old girl who grew up in a large family that engaged in crime, child abuse, sexual molestation, drug dealing, and illegal drug use. When Lulu started kindergarten and made friends, she found out other families were different from hers. She started spending a lot of time with friends' families, learning from them how healthy parenting worked. After nearly dying of pneumonia due to lack of medical care and proper nutrition at age fourteen, Lulu was taken from her family. Alice became Lulu's case manager, providing her with medical care and therapy and a happy foster family. Finally, Lulu had the life and family she had always wanted for herself.

Although the parents and three biological children in this foster family adore Lulu (she is very sweet and appealing), they are frustrated by her. Lulu insists on living not just in their world—the positive, wholesome, law-abiding world full of sports and camping trips and ballet—but also in the drug-dealing, drug-using, body-selling, alcohol-abusing world that her biological family members still live in. Though she knows she's not supposed to have contact with them, Lulu feels guilty for abandoning them and, even though she's rejected their lifestyle, doesn't want them to think she's rejecting them. Also, Lulu wants to help her flesh-and-blood siblings see how much better life is in what she calls the "nice-people" world, so they'll aspire to be part of it, too.

But, thanks to negative reinforcement from the foster family, Lulu is beginning to see she can't change her real family.

"We don't believe in using illegal drugs." "We don't drink alcohol when we're bored." "We don't go out and sell our bodies when we need money," the foster mother now says to Lulu when Lulu talks about wanting her "bio" family and foster family to get together for a barbeque on her birthday or tries to bring her sister (now a prostitute) and brother (who's addicted to crack cocaine) for visits. "I'm not saying these things are wrong, Lulu," the foster mom says firmly. "I'm saying our family doesn't do them." This is very powerful, nonjudgmental, and straightforward.

These simple statements seem to be having the desired effect. Lulu has stopped taking phone calls from her family members and stopped responding to their demands to borrow money from her. And, she's stopped trying to get her foster mom to socialize with her bio family. She has told Alice she wants the kind of values her foster family has, not just for herself but for the children she hopes to have someday.

Alice has helped the foster parents understand how much more effective it is to provide negative reinforcement of the values held by Lulu's bio family than to put down these people themselves and judge the way they live their lives.

The reinforcement of the foster family's values is helping Lulu understand what her choices are and what kind of people she values and wants to have in her life.

Using Actual Rewards as Reinforcements

Sometimes, parents need to use specific behaviors as re-inforcements. Siobhan, a suburban mother who owns her own public relations firm, says her life is too hectic for many lengthy discussions with her family. When we asked Siobhan what methods she uses to let her two teenage daughters know that they are doing well in their lives, she gave us the following list.

1. Telling them.
2. Letting them do something that they asked to do (see a movie, go to a friend's house, have a sleepover) and letting them know why.
3. Preparing their favorite food for dinner and letting them know why.
4. Getting a special treat, such as an ice-cream cone (Siobhan is rabid about the evils of junk food, so ice cream really is a treat for her girls), and letting them know why.
5. Doing something special that they haven't done in a while, such as having a fire in the chimney in the backyard, and letting them know why.
6. Giving them a hug. (Too many parents forget to provide hugs.)
7. Stating what they did well (whatever behavior Siobhan wants to reinforce) when saying good-night to them.

Notice how simple these reinforcements are. Yet all provide pleasure—if given in moderation and with sincerity.

··
When Reinforcement Becomes Dangerous

Reinforcement is such a powerful tool for influencing behavior that it must be used with care. It can be used to create snobs, racists, and intolerant human beings when overdone. If you don't think hard about what you are reinforcing in a child, you could find yourself with a child you don't enjoy at all. Here's an example of reinforcement that, though well intentioned, went wrong.

Leonie, a single mother of a son who is now grown, tells this story: "I came from a middle-class family that was loving and happy, but I envied my friend, whose parents were successful and rich, and I wanted a better life for my son. So, I always reinforced to him the value of high-class things and people and behaviors over what I considered to be low-class behaviors and people and things.

"Every time our son would bring home a friend he liked or show an interest in a relative I didn't think was high class enough, I'd say, 'That person seems nice enough, but she's not really our type.' And I'd wrinkle my nose in this way that signified distaste and sent the message, 'You can do better.'

"My husband, a machinist I loved but didn't want my son to emulate, became very annoyed with my child rearing and said I was ruining our son for life. He said I'd be sorry. We got divorced when my son was thirteen."

Leonie got her son a scholarship to an exclusive prep school, where he learned what manners to show in expensive restaurants, what brands of clothes to wear, and whom to associate with. A handsome boy with a charming personality, Leonie's son responded to her reinforcements with amazing skill. "He got into the best clique in school and got himself a scholarship to a small Ivy League college and after graduation married a girl he met there—a girl from a really wealthy family who had the same class values I did."

Sounds promising so far, right? Wrong. "The problem is," said Leonie, "I'm not high class enough for my son's wife and her family, so I'm out of their lives. The grandchildren aren't allowed to see me at all. Does my son object? Does he stand up for me? Are you high? He's been taught all too well that family loyalty is nowhere near as important a value to reinforce as social class."

Leonie's son had been made to think that people without money were negative, no matter what virtues they might have. He learned this lesson so well, he had to extrude such people—including, alas, his mother—from his life if their amount of wealth didn't measure up to his standards.

Here's another case history of a mom who didn't want her children to be poor. It has a much different ending.

This story is taken from the best-selling book *The Working Poor: Invisible in America* by David K. Shipler. It's about a woman who took the risk of not getting a job after her divorce because she knew that any job she could get would pay less than ten dollars an hour, barely enough to keep her and her children above the poverty level, and would rob her of the energy and time she needed to help the children achieve their potential in life. As a result of her not working, this mother and her children dealt sometimes with homelessness and hunger and public transportation. But this mom used her free time and energy to help her children do well in elementary and high school and to win scholarships to colleges that would develop their potential and interest—in music for her daughter, and in science for her son.

Instead of reinforcing the negative aspects of their lives, as Leonie did with her son, this mother reinforced the positive aspects of being educated. Her children became successful and fulfilled in their personal and professional lives. Both love their mother dearly for all her efforts on their behalf and make her a part of their lives today.

Some misguided (or manipulative) parents use reinforcement to make their children into what they want them to be. A former first lady decided, according to written accounts, that she did not want her handsome son to be what he reportedly wanted to be, an actor, and reinforced her desire for him to become a lawyer and a politician like the other men in his father's family. She insisted he go to law school, pass the bar exam (which was not easy for him), and work in the law field, which he tried to do.

Finally, he rebelled against the law career he obviously was not happy in by starting a political magazine. The latter project, alas, was not successful.

Reliable sources suggest that this mother also reinforced her son's choice of a wife. He eventually eschewed the flamboyant and expressive actresses he had been dating in favor of a woman who showed many of the same elegant and controlled tastes in fashion and behavior his mother exhibited. This marriage, according to magazine articles about this couple's very public and angry arguments, did not seem to go well, either.

This mother had to watch as her son's personal and professional life disintegrated more and more with every passing year, in very public ways. She passed away from cancer before this son's tragic death in an airplane accident—a death that many say he invited by flying a plane in conditions he was not trained to handle.

Reinforcing values does not mean controlling a child's life.

Should your child know what your values are? Of course. That way, your child finds out that you have values and that he can, also. Your child will eventually determine his own values; your values, however, will be what provide your child's moral and ethical foundation for the rest of his life.

Let's take time to review your values. Go back to the exercise you did at the end of chapter 1. Reread your values as though someone else wrote them. That means not judging, editing, censoring, or in any other way changing them. No "I said that? What was I thinking?" type of statements allowed.

Now, put those values away in a drawer. Wait at least twenty-four hours. Read them again and now decide which values you are happy with and which ones you want to rethink and change.

....
Reinforcing the Authentic Child

To help your child be the best she can be, use reinforcement in these ways:

- Let the child know she's got special abilities. "You are so good at organizing, Sandy. You've made that linen closet look like a darling boutique!"
- Encourage the child's healthy interests. "I see you enjoy going to the Air and Space Museum. Do you think you'd want to be a pilot someday?"
- Encourage the child to love. "You are so kind to your little sister. That is so important to her, I can tell."
- Enhance the child's natural curiosity. "You ask so many great questions. I love the way you want to learn about everything!"
- Help the child feel uniquely beautiful. "You are so interesting looking, Taylor. I have never seen such strong features; Michelangelo would have loved sculpting your face."

- Help the child feel capable. "You get that homework done, don't you? Even when it's hard, you figure out a way to do it."

You now know about modeling and reinforcing behaviors you want to exhibit in your home with consistency. On to the fourth step to having a happy home: showing rational empathy.

chapter 6

• • • • • ⊡ • • • • • •

Step Four: Using Empathy with Rational Reason

Empathizing with people means seeing their world, problems, and behavior from their viewpoint. This way of relating makes people feel validated and worthwhile. But as many experts in the rehabilitation world have pointed out, it also can cause empathizers to lose their sense of self and become martyrs. This chapter will tell how and when to use empathy with family members without losing oneself in the process.

Empathy is what you feel when you put yourself in another person's shoes. Showing empathy means letting that person know you understand why he feels as he does.

Your being able to show empathy is tremendously important to your children's mental health. One of the strongest needs people have is to be known and appreciated for themselves: as they are, intrinsically. This state of understanding between any two people is called "congruence" by Carl Rogers, a humanistic thinker who is said to be one of the most influential psychologists of all time, and "attunement" by psychiatrist Gail Saltz, M.D. In her book *Becoming Real: Defeating the Stories We Tell Ourselves That Hold Us Back,* Saltz describes attunement as "the need to be seen for who we are with acceptance."

The act of showing empathy provides a wonderful opportunity not only to find out what is going on with your child but to communicate with him about it. You can give rational reasons why you think the child's feelings may not be valid and why his behaviors may be causing him trouble. Here's an example of how this works:

Eight-year-old Mark has been yelling at everyone in the house for several days. After a big argument with his sister, Becky, one day, his mom takes him out to the gazebo and asks in a calm voice, "Mark, what's wrong? How are you feeling these days?"

"Mad!" Mark blurts out angrily. "I want people to like me, too!"

"You don't think people like you?" Mom asks.

"They only like Becky. Not me!"

Mark's perception is partly valid. His sister, Becky, has just been named state champion cheerleader and is receiving considerable attention on television, in newspapers, and from people who come over to the house to congratulate her. "It's true that Becky's getting lots of attention these days," Mom says. "I can understand why you think people like her better than you."

"I'm good, too!" Mark insists, with a pouting expression.

"You're good at lots of things. But I want you to know something."

"What?"

"People like you just as much as they like Becky. It's just that right now they are giving Becky lots of attention because she worked hard at her cheerleading and won some big prizes in cheerleading contests. Your own sister won prizes!"

"That's good," Mark says, looking slightly proud.

"But," Mom continues in the same sweet voice, "people won't like you if you keep yelling and acting all mean and mad all the time. That much I do know."

Mark is silent. He escalates his pouting.

Mom tries again. "Do you like people who yell at you? Who act all mean to you?"

"No," Mark admits, shaking his head.

Mom knows better than to belabor this point. "It's okay to feel proud of Becky. When Uncle Tom won the swimming championship, I was so proud to be his sister! It felt so good." Mom leans close now and smoothes Mark's hair from his eyes. "But I have to admit I felt a little jealous of Uncle Tom, too. Just like you feel a little jealous of Becky, huh?"

"Can we go now?" Mark asks, his face now looking smoothed and soothed. "I want to skateboard with Jim and Ray."

Does Mom stop there? No. She tells Becky why Mark has been acting like "such a brat" (Becky's words) and asks Becky if she could remember to include him a little more in her life, give him a little more personal attention. Becky says of course she will, she really loves that "little squirt" and doesn't want him feeling left out.

This example shows how parents can help children express the bad feelings that are causing unwanted behavior. Parents can show empathy for the way the child is feeling and then give rational reasons for why the child's way of expressing those feelings isn't going to work. The child then not only feels understood by other people but also finally understands why he's acting out. Children need to understand why they have the feelings they have in order to exercise some control over their behavior.

Here's another example of the use of empathy with rational reasons in a family with four teenagers:

Jim and Jerry have four girls, ages thirteen to nineteen, named for flowers—Marigold, Daisy, Lily, and Iris. Their home has always been a veritable garden full of happy girls—until Lily turned fifteen. Suddenly, she was like a kudzu plant, Jerry said, spreading her negative mood over everybody in the house. She would interrupt happy conversations with cutting comments and accuse everyone of leaving her out, not wanting her around, and making her do all the work. One day, Jim and Jerry asked Lily to go out to lunch with them. When she refused, Jim and Jerry said they would talk to her in the room she shared with Daisy. Rolling her eyes in resignation, Lily said okay, she'd go to lunch with her parents—but it had to be a place where nobody she knew was likely to see them.

At lunch, Jim said he and her mother couldn't help noticing Lily was "pretty unhappy" lately. Could she tell them what was going on with her?

"Nothing. I'm fine," Lily said, looking down at her smoothie.

"You seem to be unhappy at home," Jerry said.

"I'm fine."

"It's seems as if being with the family makes you upset," Jim said.

"Well, why wouldn't it?" Lily blurted out in a desperate tone. "Everybody but me is so nicey-nice all the time. Nobody wants to talk about anything that really matters at all—just about makeup. Boys. More makeup. Other boys. *God,* it's so frustrating."

"Can you give us some examples of what you'd like to talk about?" Jerry asked.

"It's the environment, stupid!" Lily cried. "Oh, yeah, we have a pretty yard, but look at all those pesticides you use. They're killing us! And the food you buy. God, it's so unhealthy. I know organic is more expensive, but isn't our health worth it?"

Lily's tone had become exasperated and frantic. "You're parents! You're supposed to know these things!"

To summarize the rest of this story, Jerry and Jim heard more about Lily's concerns and told her they were glad to know how she felt and what she had learned. But, they added, the way she was taking out her frustration just wasn't acceptable because it made everybody in the house uncomfortable and unhappy. They asked Lily to help plan the shopping and gardening using her knowledge about pesticides and health. They asked her to deliver a lecture on these topics one night after dinner. Lily agreed and lightened up considerably. The rest of the lunch involved education from Lily on the dangers of common pesticides that the family had always used without question.

Here's another example of rational empathy:

Harry, fourteen, is getting bad grades in algebra and French—really bad grades. He had always done fine in school until ninth grade, when his classes got harder. His parents were upset, as no one in the family (including his older sisters) had ever gotten those kinds of grades. Harry's mother, Clara, decided not to let Harry know how upset she was. Instead, she used rational empathy with him without even realizing it. "Harry," Clara said the afternoon she saw Harry's report card, "you must feel really bad about these grades. I know what a perfectionist you tend to be."

Harry just shrugged and went on playing his NBA computer game. Gently, Clara asked him to stop playing because she wanted to talk with him. When he turned off the game, he still refused to look her in the eye—or speak.

"You must be feeling like you don't belong in this family," Clara said. Not getting any kind of response from Harry, she continued on. "In this family, we don't get the kind of grades you're getting. We just don't. In some families, people do get these kinds of grades—but not in ours."

Harry looked really pained at that remark but still did not reply.

"I know you must be wondering how you can raise your grades, am I right?"

Harry nodded, tears beginning to form at the corners of his eyes.

"Do you have any ideas?" Clara asked.

Harry shook his head.

"Do you want me to give you some ideas?" Clara asked.

Harry suddenly shook his head and looked angry. "No, I don't care if my grades are bad. I just don't care."

"I can understand that you don't care," Clara went on calmly. "But you are still our child living in our family. Our family has standards in grades. That means you have to bring up the grades as soon as you can."

"No, I don't."

Clara chose to ignore this remark. "If you don't have any ideas about how to do that, I'll tell you the things we're going to do to make it happen. Do you want to hear?"

Harry gritted his teeth. But then he nodded.

"We're going to tutor you for an hour every night, starting tonight. I'll do French and Dad will do algebra. During that time, we'll make sure you understand your homework. We're also going to contact your teachers to see what else we can do. I'm looking forward to it. It'll be fun to revisit my favorite foreign language again."

"But I have band practice tonight!" Harry wailed.

"We'll try to be done before band practice," Clara said. "If you cooperate, we will be. If you don't, you'll miss band practice and maybe have to give up band till your grades improve."

"All right," Harry sighed.

Notice Harry never did explain why he got the bad grades or why he thought bad grades were okay. So, Clara told him why the bad grades were not okay—because people in their family didn't get bad grades. Maybe this reason needed some more rational explanation. But still, it was a perfectly good reason and Clara stuck to it. She told Harry what she and his dad were going to do to help him raise his grades and what would happen if Harry didn't cooperate.

Harry knows now exactly how his parents feel about his grades, what he has to do to improve the grades, and what will happen—he will have to give up his beloved band and maybe other activities as well—if he continues letting the grades slide.

Clara maintains that it was her ability to keep calm through this exchange that got her what she wanted—Harry's participation in a plan to raise his grades. "But it was so hard," she told Dr. Calmes later. "I was so mad that Harry had allowed himself to do so badly in the first place that I wanted to raise holy hell. But I know that having that kind of a fit would just make things worse." Notice that by keeping calm, Clara was also modeling the kind of behavior she wants in her home and showing that she cares about Harry very much.

The Real Problem

Easy, you say, this empathy stuff. You love knowing how your child thinks and feels. You want to know what's really going on with him. But wait. Ask yourself these difficult questions.

Do you really like your child as he is? Or do you secretly, in your heart of hearts, wish he had a different kind of personality? Are you dealing with a child who has personality traits you can't stand? Does your child, for instance, demonstrate the traits of a charmer while you prefer no-nonsense, nonschmoozing personalities? Or does she question everything you say like a detective on a TV show while what you want is a sweet little sidekick who accepts everything you say as gospel?

You must accept the personality of this child because you are not supposed to change your child's personality. You are supposed to help the child manage and develop his intrinsic personality in ways that will help him have the most fulfilled life.

Showing him that you accept his basic personality is important to his acceptance of himself. You can accomplish this important parental task by using rational empathy on yourself—remind yourself that you are happy when people are empathic with your basic personality.

You may deny that you practice rejection of your child's basic personality. Lots of parents would deny they practice this kind of rejection. But deep down, in their heart of hearts, they think such things as this: *If Billy would just be more assertive, he wouldn't get picked on so much. If Maria would just be more outgoing, she'd have more friends. If Hagar would lose some weight, she'd feel better about herself. If Joe were more persistent, he could get a better job.*

Parents often think it's their job to withhold approval of the child's basic personality until the child changes. The problem with withholding approval is that it keeps the parent from seeing the child as a satisfactory person, and thus from accepting the child as she is. This child never gets real empathy of the kind that makes her feel good enough about herself to become her own person—and to feel good about the person she is.

Ironically, children who are stars—due to some special quality such as stunning good looks, the ability to do calculus at age five, or the skill to beat all the adults at the club in racquetball—are often deprived of empathy. Many people would rather adore and admire child celebrities than care about what they really think and feel. Successful kids need empathy every bit as much as any other kid. They often feel very uncomfortable being envied and admired for extrinsic factors, such as their looks or accomplishments.

What are some specific ways to accept children as they are? One way is to find something about them—a feature, trait, or quality—that is endearing. Then, just focus on enjoying the endearing aspect. Every child has something about him that is funny, sweet, adorable, or enchanting. You can find this "something" if you try, and in trying times, you can use it to help you employ empathy. Another way is by taking an interest in a child's talent or hobby and asking questions about it. Other ways are listed later on in this chapter.

Now, let's look at two case histories showing what can happen when parents don't use rational empathy with their kids.

Nora was always a very choosy person. If something or someone was not suitable to her, she rejected that thing or person. Growing up, Nora had to have certain brands of clothing. She would not buy imitations or thrift-shop versions, and her friends had to be in the right social circles. At parties, she didn't give anyone all her attention because she was always too busy looking for someone "better" to approach. After marrying a man who was as close to perfect as she felt she could get, Nora began having children. Her fourth, a natural gymnast with movie-star looks, was the one she wanted; her other kids were allowed to fall by the wayside, deprived of the attention and resources that this fourth child received. They learned to nurture and care for one another as best they could.

As luck would have it, Nora's favored child decided not to get married. The three older children not only married but had six children among them. Today, Nora enjoys—really enjoys—these grandchildren as they are. "I just never realized how much fun, how loving, children can be," she says.

But alas. Their parents are as unconnected emotionally to their mother as she was to them. They invite her to visit with the grandchildren only a few times a year, and then only for a few hours. Their spouses' parents are the main grandparents in their children's lives, the ones who get to visit for weeks at a time and take the children on trips.

Thanks to therapy, Nora has come to understand and have empathy for the way her grown children feel. But she doesn't have the loving, accepting relationships with them she should have cultivated when they were kids. Except for her brief visits to the grandchildren, Nora doesn't see her family. Her husband divorced her when the children were in high school, and the gymnast, now an aspiring movie star, never calls.

Nora may sound unbelievable. But trust us, she's real. She's also a composite of many other parents in our society who love children not for who they are but for how they can make the parents proud.

Here's the other case history: Lewis and Arlene aspired to be in the popular clique in high school but never quite made it. They were always in that second tier, the one that operated on the fringes, as a sort of satellite to the in-group kids. Marrying soon after graduation, Lewis and Arlene did fairly well in life. They inherited Arlene's family's furniture business and ran it successfully. They had two children, a boy and girl, who were happy enough as children and seemed to like school. But when the kids reached high school, Arlene and Lewis found themselves changing. They groomed their kids to be in the in crowd, telling themselves they were doing what was best for their children. They enhanced the kids' looks with liposuction and other medical procedures that are sometimes performed on kids today. They enhanced the kids' athletic abilities with personal trainers. They "bought" the right friends for their children with gifts, trips, parties, and other enticements. When the children showed interests that Arlene and Lewis considered to be uncool, such as woodworking for the boy and jewelry making for the girl, they were told these hobbies were too "hippieish."

Arlene and Lewis had little empathy for the children's genuine interests. They assumed the children wanted the same things they had always wanted—to look great and be members of the best group in school.

Did they get their wish? Yes. The children's high school years were brilliant, making up for everything Arlene and Lewis had wanted for themselves. The boy was student council vice president and the girl was voted homecoming royalty every year and homecoming queen her senior year.

But the college years are not going so well for these kids. Never having gone to college, Arlene and Lewis have no idea how to help their children cope with college life and have, on one level, lost interest in what their children are doing. Their son is on probation in his fraternity for fighting at parties, their daughter is living with her new-age boyfriend and is pregnant, and both are doing poorly academically. Both seem to be trying desperately to figure out who they really are and what they really want. Had Arlene and Lewis had empathy for them as they really were, Arlene and Lewis could have helped them discover and learn to appreciate their real selves during some of the most important developmental years of the children's lives.

Here's a list of reasons why parents don't empathize with their kids as they really are:

- They want the children to fulfill one or more of their own unfulfilled ambitions.
- They want the children to do better than they did.
- They love being proud of their kids.
- They were not accepted by their parents and subconsciously project their pain onto their kids.
- They use images of children in the media as models, and the child thus becomes a person to be molded into a little star, not a real human being with feelings who needs empathy.

Getting to know your children as they really are will take some work on your part but can be extremely rewarding. Here are some ideas to try now:

- Schedule individual meetings with every child. These meetings should be at least a half hour long and include comfortable furniture and something tasty to eat or drink. At these meetings, have the child talk about his life. Ask questions when you want more information. Don't give your opinion unless the child asks for it. And, even then, suspend judgment as much as you can. At this meeting, tell the child about one thing he tends to say, do, or think that you like, as in, "I really like the way you are loyal to your baseball team even if you don't get to play all the time."

- Let go of the following feelings when and if you feel them: envy of other people's children, disappointment in your own children, ambition for your own children, judgment of any children for the way they look, and the desire to compare your children to other people's children. "Let go of" does not mean suppress, repress, deny, or forget these feelings. It just means let go of them. It's all right to have all the foregoing feelings; most parents in our culture have at least one of them. It's just that you can't give these feelings real power in your life. You need to disregard them when they come up if you really want happier children and a happier life for yourself.

- If you don't know what an experience is like for your child, try to imagine what it could have been like for you at your child's age. Wearing revealing clothes to school, for instance, may be an experience you never had, along with having friends whose parents are being abused, are working as strippers, are addicted to drugs, are gone so much there is almost never an adult in the home, or are unemployed. These are realities for kids of all income levels today, and your children are sure to be exposed to many of them unless they are home every minute of the day.

If one or more of these issues exists in your home, realize your kids may be getting some kind of grief for it from their friends. Be ready to empathize because your child is hurting. Children hate to be thought of as not normal in any way.

Here's our last bit of advice for showing rational empathy. Remember always, these are real people you are parenting, not unfinished pieces of pottery or paintings. They are meant to be known as the people they really are now, not by your idea of the people they should be, and helped to reach the potential they really have, not the potential you secretly want them to have.

Keep this advice in mind and watch your kids unfold in (mostly) lovely, interesting, and heartwarming ways with every passing day.

On to chapter 7, "Step Five: Caring for Animals, Plants, and Things in the Home." You'll be surprised to find out how important this seemingly all-too-obvious advice can be.

Step Five: Caring for Animals, Plants, and Things in the Home

Generally, the plants, pets, and property in a home are loved, or they would not be there. Yet, too often these possessions are neglected or disregarded in the family's busy life. This chapter will discuss why and how to care for everything in the home—and for the home itself—in ways that are pleasant, loving, and even fun.

By "caring" for animals, plants, and things in the home, we actually mean "respecting." When you show respect to animals and plants, you give them the care they need to look and be their best. You help the pet reach its full potential and develop its unique personality. You give things the polishing and cleaning and repairs they need to look their best and to last. You give plants the water, sun, and rich soil they need to thrive.

The key to success in this area is—and this is huge—that you refuse to own more plants, animals, and things than you can care for properly. This means giving away toys that are no longer used soon after they are no longer used. It means not keeping more stray kittens that find your house than you can afford to have neutered. It means having only a few thriving, glossy plants instead of a houseful in varying stages of neglect and decay.

This step means modeling respectful, loving care of plants, animals, and things with *consistency; reinforcing* family members with praise and instruction when they help with this care; and *showing rational empathy* when the children have to give up a favorite toy they no longer play with: "I know you always loved your stuffed Simbas. There's just no room in our house to keep unused toys, and other children would be so glad to get them." When it's pet bathing time, empathy might take this form: "I know you'd much rather be skateboarding, but Maxine's skin itches and smells if she's not washed at least once a week." You can even model empathy for thirsty plants when you water them every day by talking to them—"Oh, pothos, you were so dry. That water must feel so refreshing!"—stroking the leaves, and in other ways appearing to enjoy this task because you appreciate them so much.

And, this step involves matching your preferences in plants, things, and animals to the actual amounts of time, money, and skill you have for expressing those values, as well as the physical living-space needs of other family members. You might prefer a lakefront chateau furnished in Danish modern and potted hydrangeas, with a pair of pedigreed Afghan hounds having the run of the house. But you may not have the money needed to buy this kind of home or the horticultural and cleaning skills needed to maintain this kind of home, let alone keep the Afghan hounds groomed. And you may have a spouse and children who want recliners and beanbag chairs in the living room and little terrier-mix dogs from an animal shelter for pets. You need to be able to compromise your tastes for money and love.

Finally, this step is about the chores of housekeeping.

....
Teaching Your Children the Chores of Housekeeping

Many parents believe children should contribute to the care of the home, yet don't teach them how to do it. They think the children will learn on their own how to make beds, keep a tidy room, clean bathroom sinks, clear tables, and do other chores the parent assigns. In the best of all possible worlds, children will begin helping with housework on their own and do a beautiful job. But in this world, they must be told what chores you expect them to do and how to do them. If all goes well in these processes, the parents and children are mostly happily involved in the care of their home. If not, as the following case history shows all too clearly, the work of maintaining a clean, orderly home can be overwhelming and a continual source of dread.

Regan, a forty-year-old unmarried minister, is constantly battling her dread of housework. "I don't feel like I do a good job of it so I don't do it much, and then I get depressed at the way my house looks. It's like my house is saying, 'See? You can't make me look nice, so you are basically worthless.'" Realizing a year ago that her problems with housework could be signs of deeper issues, Regan went into therapy and discovered the long-repressed rage and inadequacy she felt as a child when her mother tried to make her do housework. "First of all, I never learned how to keep house. When my mother would teach me how to do something like make a bed or dry dishes, she'd get mad and say I wasn't paying attention. If I said I was paying attention, she'd say, 'You're not! I see your eyes wandering. If you don't care, I can't teach you. Do it yourself if you're so smart, and you'd better do a good job.' Then she'd storm off to leave me struggling to do the chore on my own. I never did the chore right by her standards. She'd just look at the bed I made or the dishes I was trying to dry and start crying and shaking her head. Then, she'd say in this sob-filled voice that I did such a bad job because I wanted to punish her.

"My father would comfort her and ask me why I tormented my mother so much. He'd then yell that I better finish the dishes or bed making or whatever chore was the issue, and he'd take Mom off to their bedroom to comfort her. I'd be left standing there alone, staring at their bedroom door, feeling so guilty at how I'd made my mom feel so bad." Regan stopped at this point and took a deep breath. It was her therapy, she said, that made her able to recall those childhood scenes, and doing so had been such a relief for her. "I was so happy to realize it wasn't my fault that I acted like that. I was just a kid, trying to do my best."

As a child, however, Regan was filled with a lot of fear. "I was scared my parents were right about me wanting to punish my mother, scared because I didn't know how to do a good job of the chores, and deeply exhausted from repressing the anger I was feeling toward my mother but could not acknowledge, even to myself. It was a nightmare for me that went on every day of my life until I was able to leave home.

"I know now my mother had a personality disorder," Regan continued with a sad shake of her head. "She was probably bipolar. But knowing these things doesn't make my no-good, very bad, terrible feelings about housework go away."

However, Regan said, there is hope. Thanks to her therapy, she now sees housework chores as neutral tasks that do not have to be done perfectly but will pile up if not done every day. The horror of her mother's housework-triggered tantrums is no longer retriggered when she tries to do household tasks.

Estelle, a mother of three teenage girls, said she has been so successful at teaching the art of housekeeping because her mom always modeled the satisfaction that comes from doing a chore well. "I remember her showing me how to clean the bathroom sink. She'd polish carefully in little circles and say, 'Oh, look how shiny and white that's coming. My, that's getting nice.' I loved watching her get into cleaning like that. And of course, I'd feel the same satisfaction when I tried it myself." Estelle said her mom always reinforced her efforts with positive comments, no matter how incompetently the job was done. "She'd say something like, 'You've got the right idea, Stelly, and now you're ready to learn hospital corners. They make the bed look so nice and smooth. I'll do one on this corner and then you can try on that one over there.' And so I'd learn how to make a bed well, not ever suspecting it wasn't supposed to be fun."

Estelle is glad she modeled the same attitudes and teaching techniques with her girls. "Now they not only know how to do housekeeping well, but they want to do it well. Their bedrooms are cleaner than mine."

Carrie, a mom of three teenage boys and four girls, didn't have quite so positive an experience. "My mom wasn't that great a housekeeper, and my grandmother did most of it by herself, never wanting any help. I took this course in parenting, which taught that if parents refused to do any chores around the house, the kids would do the chores themselves because they would want the house clean." Carrie shook her head at the memory.

"I'm serious, that was the premise of this lesson on chore doing. Of course, it not only didn't work; it caused terrible fights and tension so bad I stopped wanting to even be in my own home." What Carrie did that finally saved her family was implement a plan she found in one of the many books on parenting she read—which book she can't remember.

The plan involved holding a family meeting, announcing the chores that had to be done in the house and yard on a regular basis, having the kids divvy up the chores, creating a chore chart, and having the kids keep track of what chores they accomplished.

Carrie said she gave her children hints about how to do a better job if a chore was not done well, but "I absolutely refused to yell, judge, or behave in any kind of negative way. If the chore was done at all, that was enough." If the chore was not done at all, some kind of consequence would be enacted. The responsible child's allowance would be reduced. Another child would be able to do it for extra money that week. "Yes, it was a lot of record keeping at first," Carrie said. "It still is. But it's necessary.

"I tried giving up the chart system when I thought the kids were able to do the chores without it, but soon found the chore system disintegrating. After two weeks, none of the kids was doing anything—they all claimed they forgot or weren't sure what they were supposed to do."

Carrie thinks now that the structure provided by the chart system is necessary to keep her kids on task. "So it's worth the attention I give to it, even if it is sometimes more time consuming than doing a lot of the chores on my own."

As these case histories illustrate, housekeeping is not an inborn skill. It has to be learned, developed, and practiced. Finding a housekeeping system that works in your family is an important factor in carrying out Step Five. Here are some other ways to carry out Step Five:

- Polish, maintain, and display family heirlooms. Sell or give away those you don't want.
- Make art objects out of photos. Frame all photographs in your home or put them in albums. Keep the albums out where people can easily see and go through them.
- Find a charity about which your family members care. Have a meeting to discuss which charity it should be.

Get your kids accustomed to donating their unwanted possessions to that charity. Make regular donations of your unwanted things to the charity. Visit the hospitals, homes, or other facilities the charity supports on a regular basis. Reinforce the children's willingness to donate. ("That is so generous of you, Katie and Ken! Your old tennis racket will be so appreciated by kids who don't have one of their own.") And show rational empathy when the children find it hard to let go of once-treasured stuff. ("I know you could make shorts and purses out of those old jeans, Katie, but you don't have the time, we don't have the storage room, and other kids desperately need clothes.")

Why Step Five Is So Important

This step is important because it addresses concerns about managing the home. Children get panicky and frightened when they think parents can't manage the home. Contrary to what parents would like to believe, they are seldom forgiven by children when they let their homes get out of control. They are secretly resented, disparaged, and distrusted for not having better managerial skills. Their children do not remember them or their homes fondly when they grow up.

Here are some examples, taken from our interviews and experience.

Darlene's mom began collecting bride dolls when Darlene was about four years old. At first, Darlene was delighted—she adored the bride dolls, loved having so many of them displayed in her home, and was the envy of all her little girlfriends. But as Darlene got older and outgrew the dolls, she began to feel anxious. Her mother remained stuck in her need to collect them. By the time Darlene was in high school, all the shelves in the living room were lined with bride dolls, as was every available surface in the other rooms of the house. Darlene's father tried not to care and was either out at his lodge or watching television in his basement hideaway most of the time. Darlene said her mother seldom cared if the house was clean and seemed not to notice how dusty the dolls had become. "I felt the house was really intended more as a place for the dolls to live than as a place for the people who lived in it," she recalled.

Joan, a businesswoman in her forties, experienced the same feelings about her parents' Frank Sinatra memorabilia collection when she was growing up. "Every object in our house, from the rugs to the ceiling fixtures, had Frank's signature or photo on it. It was like living in a museum devoted to the memory of Frank." Even the guest bathroom accessories— soap dish, shower curtain, hand towels—bore Sinatra insignia of one kind or another. "I know that's hard to believe," Joan said, "but it's true. My mother got catalogues advertising all kinds of things decorated with Frank Sinatra's signature or photo."

Was Joan amused at her parents' decor? "I was embarrassed. Friends who came over were always making fun of my house. They'd say things like, 'I bet your mom could find toilet paper with Frank's picture on it,' and I'd pretend to laugh along with them, but inside I'd want to die."

These examples provided by Darlene and Joan indicate the need children have for a sense of belonging in the home. That means feeling as if the home is as much theirs as it is the parents' home. Plants, animals, or things associated with one family member's hobby should be confined to one room and not be allowed to take over common living areas. Parents' collections should not usurp attention and space belonging to other family members. Everyone's trophies should be displayed in the family room, not just those of the family star athlete.

The parents in these examples might have had addictions not just to the objects they collected, the bride dolls and Sinatra products, but also to collecting itself. True, such addictions may not be in the same class as addiction to heroin or alcohol or other ingested substances, but they do qualify as addictions in the sense that they adversely impact the lives of family members.

Noreen's story shows what can happen in the home if parents don't address their addictions to alcohol. Noreen remembered her parents always saying they were going to stop drinking alcohol. "They didn't have jobs because they were trust-fund babies. They had more money than they knew what to do with. We lived in a mansion with almost no furniture except for a banquet-sized table in the dining room, an in-home theater with leather sofas and chairs in the entertainment room, and waterbeds in their bedroom and mine," Noreen recalled. "Every morning, my parents would sit at the dining-room table with their hangovers, trying to drink coffee but not really eating any of the food the cook made for them. They would say they were going to give up alcohol, go to Twelve Step meetings, go out to buy furniture and plants, and see about taking in foster children because our house was so huge for just the three of us."

Noreen recalls how happy she would feel at these breakfast meetings. "I'd always be so excited because I loved plants and wanted lots of furniture, and, of course, I was dying to have brothers and sisters. But then, by about 10:00 A.M., my parents would start planning dinner for that night. Usually it was too complicated for our cook to prepare, so they'd call a caterer and order this sumptuous dinner to be brought in.

"By about 11:30, my parents would start to drink wine, and I'd get worried. I'd worry that they weren't going to buy the furniture, that they were going to stay home as they always did, watching movies and drinking wine and calling people up to invite them over for dinner. It was terrible to worry about being so disappointed and then to actually be disappointed, but that was the story of my life till I was able to go to school and think about something else."

By the time the dinner guests would come over, at about 4:00 in the afternoon, Noreen's parents were always "very high." The alcoholic drinks and other intoxicating substances (which Noreen to this day refuses to identify) were served in such abundance that the food was largely forgotten. "I would eat this elegant food all by myself every night, in my room, until I was no longer hungry. Then I'd be put to bed by my nanny. She wasn't a live-in, and she always looked worried when she left me at night to go home. She'd say, 'Don't go out there, you hear? Just go to sleep now, and morning will be here before you know it.'"

The trust funds eventually ran out, the mansion was sold at a loss, Noreen's parents divorced, and both are now sober and remarried. "If they had just tried to make a nice home for me, just bought the furniture they always promised they were going to buy, it wouldn't have been so bad," Noreen said, her voice breaking and her eyes filling with tears. She is still re-living those childhood scenes. Noreen's therapist is urging Noreen to attend Twelve Step meetings—preferably ACA (Adult Children of Alcoholics) meetings. ACA, which is meant for children of any age whose parents are or were addicted to alcohol or other substances, may help Noreen separate herself from her parents, process those childhood memories, and go on to live her own life. Though Noreen does not drink or use drugs herself, she remains in part the little girl living in an empty house; she still gets very depressed when she has to buy furniture for her apartment. Not wanting to go through the possible "hassles" of having roommates, Noreen lives by herself in a studio apartment, has no social life to speak of outside of her job, and struggles with extreme feelings of loneliness every day of her life.

Zelda, a devoted member of ACA, recalls being relieved when her cocaine-addicted parents got "busted" by the police. "We had no furniture left by that time except a rickety old filthy couch and a TV that seldom worked. Everything else had been sold or bartered for drugs.

"We had all these pets our parents would bring home when they were high that never got fed. Our parents never bought the food to feed them. The only thing I wanted to know from the social worker who took us away was if the pets would now get enough to eat."

Jan recalls a childhood spent trying to get her alcoholic mom to care about the apartments they lived in. "I'd buy things at thrift stores like doilies and dresser scarves to cover the burns and scratches," she remembered. Jan was so excited when her mother and her mother's boyfriend bought a thoroughbred standard poodle. "It meant my mother cared about something and that I had a pet that she and I could care about together." The mother and the boyfriend stopped drinking and bought books on dog breeding. They created a space for the dog with blankets and dog toys and pillows. They had the poodle bred and sold the resulting five puppies for a good amount of money. "I was ecstatic," Jan said. "My mom had been sober for so long and seemed to love dog breeding."

Three days after the puppies had been sold, Jan woke up to find all the puppies back in the house, yelping and hungry and "going to the bathroom all over the place." Jan found her mom and the boyfriend passed out in her mom's room. "I found out later that the two of them had gotten drunk and decided they wanted the puppies back. They'd gone to every home where a puppy lived and kidnapped the puppy; they literally stole all the puppies." The police knew where to look for the stolen puppies. Jan, then twelve, was put in foster care. She loved her foster family and thrived under their care. After graduating high school, she went on to become a Chinese acupuncturist and massage therapist. She attends Al-Anon regularly because her mother continues to binge drink and, to this very day, demands that Jan spend more time with her and loan her money.

Almost every child of addicted parents has similar stories to tell.

Parents don't have to be substance abusers to have poor home management skills. Claudia's mother was a widowed artist who couldn't be bothered to clean the home, water the plants, and care for the many ferrets the family loved. "My mother actually sold her art. She did paintings to order to match people's decor when we needed money," Claudia said. "She expected my two sisters and me to do the housework and pet care and plant watering, but she never taught us how to do it." A believer in progressive education, this mother told her children that whatever they wanted done, they would learn how to do. If they wanted the house kept up, they would learn how to do it. "But we never did learn how," Claudia said. "I know now we were too angry at our mother to learn how to do those things we thought she should know how to do."

Jonah's mother was simply "an incompetent housekeeper. My dad would yell at her about her poor housecleaning and finally left her and married a woman who kept an immaculate house. Mom loved my brother and me and got custody, but it was very hard for us to come back home after being in the clean, orderly house Dad lived in with his new wife."

Jonah's mother eventually hired a housekeeper who not only cleaned but also taught Jonah's mother how to organize and clean the house. "Mom never did get as good at housekeeping as Dad's new wife. But it was the fact that we could see her making an earnest effort to improve that won our hearts." Jonah said he and his brother also learned from this housekeeper how to help keep the house well maintained. "It was really good for us. Dad's new wife always did everything—picked up after us and spoiled us rotten. That wasn't good for us at all."

Jonah said his mom always called the housecleaner "my housekeeping therapist" and agrees that this is what that woman actually was. "She knew we had issues about cleaning and housekeeping and helped us learn how to deal with those issues and the house ourselves."

Beware of becoming too dependent on hired help to care for the home. You can hire a person to do the heavy, basic cleaning if you can't manage it. But you still need to be showing the care of the plants, pets, and things yourself. That's because your family needs to see you modeling that caring connection with the family's things, pets, and plants on a consistent basis.

More Reasons Why Caring for Pets, Plants, and Things in the Home Matters So Much

Children whose parents neglected this step may have problems creating the kinds of homes they want for their families when they move out and set up housekeeping on their own. "My home is like a motel suite," says Carl, a divorced economics professor. "The only things I allow in it are impersonal expensive objects, all in shades of black and white and maybe now and then a spot of blue. My ex-wife was a pack rat who brought home boxes of stuff from yard sales every weekend and piled it up and left it. She always said that it'd get used or given as gifts or sold, but it never did." Carl didn't know his wife was a pack rat when he married her. But, as so often happens, she turned out to have a lot of the same acquiring and hoarding tendencies as his mother.

"My mother thought she had to own every single object left in the world that was made in the 1940s and 1950s," Carl recalled. "She spent every spare moment at flea markets and swap meets and estate sales. My dad usually went with her; they'd live in their Winnebago if the sale was out of town. My sister always went with them, but not me. I hated that life with a passion."

Carl says he loves his parents but hates to go visit them at their home. "It's like they care more about their stupid stuff than they do me," he says. "I guess I've always felt that way, but I'm just now able to say it."

Carl misses being married to his wife and hopes to reconcile with her. They have discussed her pack-rat problem and the effect it had on their relationship. However, they are not going to jump into remarriage quickly. They've decided to seek counseling as a couple before sharing a home again—they hope the counseling will help them be able to create a home that reflects both their personalities and tastes and is a place they can both enjoy.

Joyce attributes her breast cancer partly to the fact that her mother had all her clothes—even her simplest play clothes and cotton dresses—dry-cleaned after one wearing from the time she was two years old till she was in high school. "Mom worked about seventy hours a week as an architect and wanted me looking nice for day care, then pre-nursery school, then nursery school, then kindergarten and elementary school and junior high. I would automatically put my clothes in the dry-cleaning pile every single day when I came home. I know Mom was busy, but she could have taken some time to find out if the chemicals used in dry cleaning were really safe for kids."

And failure to care properly for the pets, plants, and things in the home can lead to tragedy of the worst kind a parent can imagine. A worst-case example? Loaded guns left where children can find them can lead to a child's death.

Several cases of this sort tell the same sad story: An older child is visiting. Wanting to impress this older person, a boy living in the home tells him he knows where the family's gun is kept and will show it to him. In the process of holding the gun, one boy pretends to aim it at the other and shoots. The gun actually does go off at that point and kills, or permanently injures, the other child.

This story has many variations but almost always the same common characteristics: The children involved are boys, and the parents of the shooter always believe the child had no idea where the gun was, or else knew but had been trained well enough to know he shouldn't use the gun to show off.

Had the parent been attending carefully to Step Five, he or she might not have left a loaded gun in an accessible place or had a loaded gun in the house at all.

Enough sad stories involving Step Five. Let's move on to some happy ones.

Happy Step Five Stories

Arnold's father did all the cooking at their house because Arnold's mother did not enjoy cooking. Now Arnold does more housework in his home than any other husband his wife knows. "You must have taught him right. He doesn't bat an eyelash when it comes to cleaning and cooking and changing babies," Arnold's wife tells Arnold's mother, now a widow, every time Arnold's mother comes to visit.

Arnold's mother just smiles and says she did her best. The truth is, she valued Arnold's father's contributions to the home—especially his cooking—and let him and everyone else in the family know it all the time.

During the occupation of France in World War II, Martine's mother learned about home decor when there was almost nothing in France to decorate with. "Oh, the French," Martine said with a fond smile. "What they can do with a bare shelf and a single objet d'art, maybe a tiny blooming weed in an empty glass bottle. It's not to be believed." Martine, a talented amateur photographer, practices the same minimalist decor principles in her home, using only those objets d'art made by her children. "Children are natural Picassos, you know, and Pollocks and also Rodins."

As a result of her careful displays, her children have become ever more creative. One is an architect and the other two work as graphic designers. The architect remembers how life was with Martine. "I think my favorite memory is how my mother would not just take photos of us children, but photos of us with our favorite things.

"We had to drag all our favorite toys outside and surround ourselves with them. The arranging would take what seemed like hours but the results always made me feel so special, like I had so much meaning, somehow. I think having my favorite things in the photo gave more meaning not just to the objects but to me."

Caring for things, as well as animals and plants, helps a happy home happen. But we also must care for the people in the home, which brings us to chapter 8, Step Six. There are many more ways of caring for family members than you'd think—many of which will, when practiced, keep your home overflowing with love and goodwill.

chapter 8

•••••• ▣ •••••

Step Six: Caring for All the People in the Home

Let's start this chapter with a question: Whose job is it to care for the people in your family—yours or theirs? Answer: It's your job. There. We could end this chapter right here because that answer says it all.

But, we'll elaborate for a few pages because we want you to understand *why* it's your job to care for people in your family and *what* happens when parents don't assume this job. We also want you to know how practicing the other five steps in the Big Six makes this step easy and fun.

••
Why Caring for the People in Your Family Is Your Job

You're a parent. Parents care for one another and for the children. What is caring? It's the expression of love for someone by performing lots of separate acts for that person. As for what those acts might consist of, we like the list suggested by famed pediatrician-turned-psychoanalyst D. W. Winnicott. According to Winnicott, the "good-enough mother" (or parent) nurtures, organizes, responds empathically, absorbs attacks from children, and does not retaliate. Especially important to

Winnicott is the act of mirroring—saying what the child says ("You are thirsty!") and appearing to feel what the child feels—as in saying "Ooooh, you're sad!" in a sad voice with a sad-looking expression when looking at the child who looks sad. Winnicott believed that the act of mirroring tells the child he exists and that his existence is a good thing.

We also like the idea that caring for a child is forming an attachment with her. With American psychologist Mary Ainsworth, English psychiatrist John Bowlby developed this notion into his famous theory of attachment in the 1980s. We'll explore this theory a bit more in a moment.

What Happens to Children When Parents Don't Really Care for Them

Children who aren't cared for properly tend to suffer emotionally. They may be successful financially and career-wise, but deep down, they are likely to sustain an emotional emptiness that can adversely affect their relationships. How do we know about this effect? We consulted Joyce Selenkow, MA, LAC, a family therapist who has practiced in Los Angeles and is now in Arizona. Here is her response:

> Just as behaviors are learned, emotional patterns can be learned, also. If a child is neglected emotionally, that pattern of feeling emotional emptiness follows him into adulthood. It becomes a part of him that, if not pleasant, is still comfortable, like an old shoe. There is also a setup for failure in the child's future relations. The child probably never learned how to give in an emotionally healthy way, and so has always taken too much from others instead of giving. One tends to replay what one is emotionally familiar with, even a negative, empty feeling.

Studies of college students support this answer from Joyce Selenkow. Researchers found that those students who had had strong early attachments with their caregivers had fulfilling relations in their college lives, while those who did not had problems making friends and felt unfulfilled and lonely. Outcomes of the hundreds of attachment-theory studies conducted from the 1980s to the present all suggest that most adults with the inability to connect to others were not lovingly attached to their caregivers in childhood.

An article on attachment theory in *Mothering* magazine says that this theory is "based on the belief that the mother-child bond is the essential and primary force in infant development and thus forms the basis of coping, negotiation of relationships and personality development."* But, says Lauren Lindsey Porter, the author of this article, the need for attachment continues past infancy. The older child needs to reattach to Mom (or whoever the primary caregiver is) every now and then in order to deal with problems and difficulties with other people. Porter says not to worry about periods of misattachment with the child, when the parent and child do not see eye to eye and are not getting along. If not allowed to go on too long before reattaching takes place, these periods can strengthen the child, making her more resilient in handling relationship problems in other areas of her life.

How does a parent attach to a child? By responding to the child in positive, affectionate ways, Porter says. We say that by implementing the Six Steps every day, the parent will automatically attach to kids—in many positive ways.

Enough academic grounding. Here's a real example of how poor attachment in childhood leads to lack of loving relationships in later life: Aristotle Onassis. Abandoned by his parents

---

* Lauren Lindsey Porter, *Mothering,* no. 119 (July/August 2003).

as a very small child, he raised himself without having anyone to give him any real care. Despite his ability to create great wealth, he was unable to sustain relationships with wives and mistresses and often treated them badly. He kept opera singer Maria Callas in a state of limbo for over a decade, having her believe he would marry her and allegedly persuading her to abort their child when she became pregnant by him. Then, suddenly, he left her for Jacqueline Kennedy—whom he did marry. Devastated by the loss of Onassis and the child, Callas reportedly went into a deep depression, from which she never really recovered.

Onassis's legacy of emotional emptiness was apparently passed on to his daughter, Christina. Despite being one of the wealthiest women in the world, she was unable to sustain a loving relationship with a man. After her breakup with the man considered to be the love of her life, the father of her daughter Athina, she died in what may have been a suicide at the age of thirty-seven. This example illustrates the fact that money—all the money in the world—cannot buy the kind of caring a child needs in order to have fulfilling relationships in later life.

When Lots of Parents Stopped Caring about Kids—A Brief History Lesson

In the late 1960s, the country's divorce rate took a sharp turn upward that peaked in 1979 at about 50 percent of all first marriages (higher for subsequent marriages) and has hovered between 40 percent and 50 percent ever since. Parents who would never have considered divorce in the 1950s were now dissolving their legal and emotional ties. Social historian Barbara Dafoe Whitehead said in her book entitled *The Divorce Culture: Rethinking Our Commitments to Marriage and Family* that in this period of the soaring divorce rate, divorce suddenly became morally permissible, socially sanctioned, and a sign of growth in the person initiating the divorce. Children were believed to be resilient enough to handle divorce.

Not only parents but also therapists, psychologists, and medical doctors believed kids would be happier if their parents were fulfilled in life. Not to think this way was to be hopelessly old-fashioned and afraid to live life to the fullest.

The truth was, as Berkeley professor Judith S. Wallerstein discovered in her twenty-five-year-long study of children of divorce reported in her groundbreaking book, *Surviving the Breakup: How Children and Parents Cope with Divorce,* many of those children felt unloved, frightened of what the future would hold, and, sadly, that their parents just didn't care about them anymore, at least not in the ways they needed to feel cared for. They were sustaining losses of people they loved, along with emotional (and sometimes physical) neglect from people they still had in their lives. Also, they had trouble maintaining intimate relationships in their adolescent and adult years because they saw breaking up as the only cure for disagreements and fights.

Divorce is not quite so devastating for most children today—that's because we know so much more about their reactions to divorce and are far more sensitive to their pain. We also know a lot more about children in general and the kind of care they need.

Many parents, however, don't know right care from wrong care because they've never learned the differences. The following sections will help clarify those differences.

The right kind of caring is not just a matter of scheduling dental and medical appointments and making sure the kids are well fed, bathed, and groomed. It's a matter of understanding their emotional and physical needs—and putting those needs before yours. The child is not, in other words, responsible for soothing you when you feel bad. You are responsible for soothing your child. That is how your child eventually learns how to soothe herself when she is upset. Children raised to worry about how Mom is feeling never learn how to understand and handle feelings of their own.

It's also a matter of understanding that your child still needs your caring, no matter how independent and self-sufficient she may seem.

So far in this chapter, we've discussed good kinds of caring. But there are bad kinds, also, that parents need to understand and try to avoid.

The Misuse of Children by Adults— How to Avoid the Temptation

Providing the wrong kind of care involves misusing children. We're not just talking about incest here, although incest is certainly one of the most destructive misuses of children. We're talking about a parent's subconscious misuse of children. This includes the following behaviors:

- Taking out feelings such as rage, desire, resentment, and self-pity on a child.
- Expecting the child to live out parental dreams.
- Telling the child lies.
- Having the child act as parent to the parent.

Parents are often unaware, or in denial, that they misuse their children in these ways. The main reason parents resort to these practices is that they are not getting their own needs met and, in the case of some parents, have never gotten their needs met.

To find out if you might be indulging in these destructive parental practices, take the following quiz. Just answer yes or no to every question.

1. Do you ever have bouts of sobbing and sadness in front of your child?
2. Do you bad-mouth or gossip about people with your child?
3. Do you insist that your child's friends be in a certain social class or be a member of a special social clique or sports team?
4. Do you ask your child to go shopping with you for clothes or to the hairstylist so he can approve your new outfit and hairdo?
5. Do you overlook unwanted behaviors in your child's friends because you want your child to have these friends?
6. Do you seek your child's comfort and counsel when you are feeling upset?
7. Do you compete with your child's friends' parents to have the best birthday parties, the best baby and wedding showers, the cutest-dressed kids?
8. Do you tell your child lies about yourself and your family for any reason at all?
9. Do you tell your child why you like, admire, or enjoy one of her siblings or a child outside the family better than you do her?
10. Do you blame other adults in your child's life—teachers, friends' parents, coaches, and counselors—for everything wrong in your child's life?
11. Does your status as parent make you feel secretly smug and superior to your or your spouse's family members?
12. Do you tell your child his existence has robbed you of the chance for a happy life?

Answering yes to three or more of these questions means you may be misusing your child. Now let's go back and look at rationalizations for these methods of misuse and reasons why they are not valid.

Do you ever have bouts of sobbing and sadness in front of your child?

You tell yourself that it's okay to show the child that parents have feelings, also. The truth is, it's not okay to make the child feel bad if you feel bad. The child will then think she's responsible for making you feel better, and no child should have to shoulder that responsibility for a parent, ever.

Do you bad-mouth or gossip about people with your child?

You tell yourself that your child should know about the people who hurt you and are mean to you. The truth is, the child needs to feel you are strong enough, and wise enough, to be able to handle these kinds of people without letting them get you down. He needs to know the truth about people—that Cousin Bob is now in prison for drug dealing or Aunt Helen has temper tantrums that are not appropriate in public—but he does not need, and should never be asked, to take sides.

Do you insist that your child's friends be in a certain social class or be a member of a special social clique or sports team?

You tell yourself the child should have nice friends from nice families. True. But teach your child to choose friends on a superficial basis, and she'll become shallow and superficial in ways you won't like at all. She should be encouraged to choose friends on the basis of qualities—such as honesty, loyalty, and shared interests—that money cannot buy.

Do you ask your child to go shopping with you for clothes or to the hairstylist so he can approve your new outfit and hairdo?

You tell yourself your child loves having his opinion asked about your clothes and hairstyle. The truth is, he wants parents who can think for themselves—even if he doesn't like how they look. And he'll feel secretly uncomfortable because (children are very perceptive about these matters) he'll worry he's expected to evaluate how attractive you are to romantic partners—and that should never be his job.

Do you overlook unwanted behaviors in your child's friends because you want your child to have these friends?

You tell yourself it's none of your business if your child's friends do things you don't approve of. But as long as your child associates with these friends, it *is* your business. Your child really wants you to help her decide which behaviors are acceptable and which ones are not. You don't have to judge or label these friends as bad people; just let your child know that their behaviors and/or activities are not acceptable.

Do you seek your child's comfort and counsel when you are feeling upset?

You tell yourself your child wants to make you feel better when you are sad. Maybe so, once in a while. But on a constant basis, this responsibility makes the child feel trapped—also insecure and frightened.

Do you compete with your child's friends' parents to have the best birthday parties, the best baby and wedding showers, the cutest-dressed kids?

You tell yourself your child wants to be proud of the parties you give. The truth is, parents who try too hard to impress their children's friends or their friends' parents or anyone else embarrass children. Kids know when their parents have spent money they do not have on a party, and so do the other children attending. (How do they know? Trust us, they have built-in radar.) Children respect parents who stay within their means. (No, they won't tell you this, but they do.)

Do you tell your child lies about yourself and your family for any reason at all?

Think how you feel when you find out you've been lied to. Now realize that children feel all these feelings magnified because the parent is their whole world. If the parent lies, who else is lying to them? Who can be trusted? And don't think your lies to your children won't be found out—they almost always are. You yourself will want the child to know the truth when the child is mature enough to hear it, because maintaining the lies will begin causing you a great deal of emotional pain.

Do you tell your child why you like, admire, or enjoy one of her siblings or a child outside the family better than you do her?

You tell yourself that comparing your child to others will encourage her to try harder in life. Instead, it will make your child feel unloved, discouraged, and depressed.

Do you blame other adults in your child's life— teachers, friends' parents, coaches, and counselors— for everything wrong in your child's life?

You want your child to see you as the tiger or tigress protecting his or her young, taking on anyone who criticizes your kid in any way. Instead, you are teaching your child that other people are always to blame for his shortcomings, that finding someone, anyone, to blame is all he has to do to get through life, and that he never has to be accountable for himself.

Does your status as parent make you feel secretly smug and superior to your or your spouse's family members?

Some families make a very big fuss over members who reproduce the family bloodlines. The truth is, you need to parent your child, not just bask in the attention her birth has bestowed upon you.

Do you tell your child his existence has robbed you of the chance for a happy life?

You tell yourself your child will be glad to know how much you had to sacrifice for him. But the child will not be glad to know this information—he will feel awful and guilty. If you still resent the child for stopping that budding concert pianist career in its tracks, remember this: Your child did not ask to be born, especially not to you, and your child did not have to be kept by you—he could have been adopted by any number of loving parents who can't have children of their own.

By now, you might understand better that misusing children in the foregoing ways really pleases the parent at the children's expense. If you find yourself resorting to any of these or other misuses, get therapy. We advise psychotherapy instead of counseling because therapy gets at the root causes of these behaviors that can hurt your children so much. Also, take a parenting class or form a support group with other parents, using one of these twelve ways of misusing children as a basis of discussion every time you meet.

Now, let's examine the positive ways of caring for your children and other people in your family using the steps in the Six Step Plan.

Modeling Caring for Family Members

Put yourself in positive "caring" mode. That means pausing and taking time to realize how much love, appreciation, enjoyment, and gratitude you have for your family members and letting yourself experience these wondrous feelings. Think, if you can, how devastated you would be if suddenly they were no longer in your life. Let yourself be grateful, so grateful, you still have them all. When you're in this frame of mind, you'll automatically model love and caring as you pursue your regular parenting tasks.

Show caring to family members and others in the home and to family members outside the home. Visit or call relatives in nursing homes; make care packages of hand-me-downs for relatives who are poor. If you don't have relatives in need of caring, find other people outside your home who do, such as children who have been taken from their parents because of violence. Make sure your children see you provide this caring for people outside the home on a regular basis. You can ask them to participate with you after you have modeled this behavior on your own with consistency for a few months.

Reinforcing Family Members When They Respond to Your Caring

When you reinforce positive responses to your caring, you help others feel good about caring. "What a nice hug," you say when you get hugged back. Or, "You make me feel special" when a child does something nice for you or anyone else. Or, "You take such good care of your clothes (or your pets or little sister)." Or, "I am so happy you want to go with me when I visit Aunt Nell in the nursing home. It makes it so much more fun to show her the caring she needs when you come along. And it shows her you care, also."

Showing Consistency in Your Caring

This step means regulating your mood. You don't just care for your family when you're in a good mood and they're in a good mood and you're not tired. You've seen parents who pick up their children from day care centers giving only a minimum of a greeting, walking silently to their cars with the child's hand in theirs, looking grimly ahead—not connecting with the child emotionally at all. Yes, these parents are probably tired and upset about something that happened at work. But they still need to show the child that they are glad they can care for him again, after having had to be away from him all day.

It doesn't take much work to show consistent caring for your family. You can do it all the time in little ways—by smiling, hugging, and acting glad to be in their company. You can say, "I'm a little too tired to cook, so let's have big salads. I'll chop the veggies, and you can shred the lettuce." But saying something such as, "I'm too tired. I shouldn't have to cook all the time. You're old enough to make dinner more often," only makes others feel guilty or resentful and think that meal preparation is just one big drag they'll never do if they don't have to.

Reinforcing Children When They Show Caring

If a child is expected to care for her dog, and she does it, she doesn't need praise. But she does need to be acknowledged for doing the job adequately. "This dog seems so happy," you can say. "He looks loved and well cared for." Or, if the child shows caring for a sibling, you can say, "I love knowing you will get your little sister into her shoes every morning so they'll be tied properly and she won't trip on her laces. That is just such a big worry off my mind." The key is to avoid stock "praise" phrases and words such as "Good job!" "Wow, that's terrific!" and "Keep up the good work!" because they begin to sound automatic and meaningless and manipulative after just the second or third use. Children and other people know when they're getting "one size fits all" kinds of attention, and they dislike it intensely—because they know it's not recognizing who they really are.

Showing Rational Empathy When Caring for the People in Your Home

All you have to do in this step is ask questions. That's the fun part. But you need to know what kinds of questions to ask in order to show you really care about the person you're questioning.

The questions cannot be

- Too general, as in "How was school today?" Of course the child is going to give a one-word answer—"Okay" or "Fine" or "Terrible." General questions get general answers.
- Too personal, as in "How's that girl in your Spanish class you said you had a crush on?" Or, "Do you have any boyfriends in your classes?"
- Too perfunctory, indicating you don't really want an answer. "So, how are your classes going?" "Do you think your football team has a chance this year?" Or, as one girl's mother would ask her whenever she came home from college, "How's President Pacheco (the president of the college) doing?"
- Too negative, indicating anger or disapproval. "Have you finally figured out how to get along with your

friends, Donnie?" "Michelle, where did you get the money for those nails? You didn't go to one of those cheap nail places that give you funguses, did you?" "Martin, I want to know the truth. Are any of those people you hang out with not on drugs? They all look like they are." And, "Vance, do you care more about those video games than you do your own parents? Come on, tell me, right now!"

- Too much about you. "Do you like this dress I'm wearing?" "Should I change jobs?" Or, "Do you think I should divorce your dad?"

To show rational empathy, questions should

- Make sense, such as, "Are you able to get your homework done working so many hours at your job?"
- Get the child or family member to think for himself. "Would you rather spend your spare time on piano lessons or tennis?" Or, "Which do you like better, tennis or piano? Or do you like them both the same?"
- Lead to thoughtful discussions. The piano versus tennis question is likely to provide a good conversation. "If you could pursue only one of them, which do you think would do you the most good, piano or tennis?"
- Indicate you find this person intellectually interesting. "How are you able to spend so much time on your 4-H projects and still do well in school?" "Can you tell me how you are able to remember so much of what you read?"
- Show your belief that the child is justified in her behavior. "I know Uncle Tom is often offensive in his personal table manners. Is that why you won't eat dinner with us if he's a guest?" Or, "You told me you were

not able to get along with your math teacher. Is that a reason why you got a D this period?"

- Show caring for pets, plants, and things. Showing love for people's plants, pets, and things is showing love for the owners. You help your son feed his rabbits; you help your daughter catalog her CDs. You help your children grow their avocado trees from avocado pits. You admire the pets, plants, and things they own and admire. If the child owns something you don't allow in your house, such as pornographic videos and weapons, you put them in a box and tell him he can't have these things until he leaves your home for good. Get his opinion on how these things should be disposed of—you can suggest he put them in a bank safe-deposit box to which you will hold the key and he makes payments or that he find another way to dispose of them properly. (Then you use rational empathy to find out why he brought these things into your house and why he likes them, and then tell him why you do not. Your rational reasons can include the facts that the items involve hurting and disrespecting people.) Find ways to display children's arts and crafts in the living room and other common areas, instead of confining them to their rooms.

So much for the Six Steps and the ways in which they can be used separately and in combinations with each other to help you show caring for all the people in your home. These steps will take practice, at first, especially if your home now reflects your family members' bad moods, resentments, fatigued silences, and lack of meaningful talk. But if you keep at these steps for your own sake, without expecting changes in behaviors from anyone else, you'll soon find them becoming contagious in their positive effects. You'll be enjoying yourself and other family members so much, you'll find your home a great place to be.

This ends the chapters explaining the use of the Six Steps. Now on to chapter 9, "How the Six Steps Contribute to Kids' Growth."

chapter 9

•••••• ▣ ••••••

How the Six Steps Contribute to Kids' Growth

Children who are thriving emotionally, intellectually, physically, and spiritually are joys to have around. This chapter will explain why kids thrive in a happy home and fail to thrive in an unhappy home.

Going from one developmental stage to another requires children to face many new challenges. These stages can be viewed broadly in terms of ethical values.

How Children Grow

From birth through six months, the child values himself and his ability to get himself the food, comfort, and affection he needs by crying and cooing and through other behaviors that bring the desired response.

From six months through three years, the child values others as separate people who are interesting and helpful.

From three through five, the child values people for social purposes because playing is now a major focus of her life. The child also values people as sources of information who can satisfy her insatiable curiosity. Parents are now enjoyed for both purposes and serve as role models for, and guides to, getting along with people.

From five through eight, the child values teachers and other authority figures outside the family for the structure and order and instruction they bring to his life.

From eight through twelve, the child values peers for camaraderie and status and peer mentoring.

From twelve through eighteen, the child values others for their romantic appeal—and for the support they provide (as in friendship) in pursuing people who are romantically desirable.

From eighteen to twenty-four, the child values those who can help her pursue such adult goals as preparing for and entering a career and finding a mate.

From twenty-four on, the child will, if he is behaving as nature intended, value babies because he wants one or more of his own.

Of course, these developmental stages vary with every individual child. But on the whole, these stages prioritize what most children value through the course of their lives.

The child is not expected to drop the people she valued in previous stages when she enters new stages; she goes on valuing the "old" people but stops giving them as much emphasis in her life.

If these stages seem as though they are just nature's plan to perpetuate the species and provide for our young, you are right. But if you think it's easy for children to go from one of these stages to another, you're wrong.

Look back on your own life. Remember all the conflicts, divided loyalties, decisions about who gets to stay in your life and who gets dropped, and all the fears you had about how you were going to do in the next stage? Remember wondering if you'd be successful at all the new tasks you had to accomplish and if you'd be able to cope; if you would be able to make new friends and if those friends would like you? And later on, if someone you were attracted to would find you desirable? And if you'd be able to find a spouse willing to be a coparent for the family you wanted to start or a good boss who would teach you what you needed to know for your career?

Mastering the transitions from one stage to another requires that children grow emotionally, intellectually, physically, and spiritually. Children must learn how to deal with and regulate unfamiliar emotions they'll experience in the new stage; learn the concepts and information necessary for succeeding in the new stage (such as algebra rules in adolescence and job skills in adulthood); develop the stamina and coordination necessary for the new life stage; become comfortable with the bodily changes that happen in the new life stage; and find a satisfying spiritual source of some kind to rely on.

All growth produces anxiety to some extent. And that anxiety is so much more manageable if the child grows up in a happy home. Here's why:

The happy home provides security, a base of confidence that eases anxiety. The happy base includes people who care about the child, who encourage consistency in efforts to pursue his goals, who model persistence in the face of obstacles, who reinforce his determination to succeed, who empathize with his despair when he has setbacks, and who make sure he has the things he needs—such as the right clothes, education, and supplies—to help him succeed.

As a result of this base, the child is able to adjust well to all the settings of his life stages—school, sports, social circles, and job—with a degree of confidence. The child knows he will fail at times but has the coping skills to get through difficult times.

Here's a case history showing how families help children who are having a hard time with a life stage transition:

Gloria grew up in a family of seven that was very happy, boisterous, and supportive. Gloria was always the "bookish" child who loved literature courses. When all nineteen of Gloria's applications to doctorate programs in English literature were turned down, Gloria's family never even thought of letting Gloria give up her dream of becoming an English professor in a college. Failure just wasn't an option they would let Gloria consider.

Her parents and siblings suggested she talk to one of her undergraduate teachers and have him intervene with one of the colleges on her behalf. Gloria took this advice and did find an undergrad professor willing to call a few admissions officers at the colleges to which Gloria was applying and tell them how qualified she was. Within a week, Gloria got an offer of admission and a teaching assistantship to a respected university in the Southwest. Because of the caring support of her family, Gloria is now very happily studying and gaining experience for her future career.

The child growing up in a happy home thrives emotionally because she is emotionally healthy—she feels good about herself most of the time. She cares enough about herself to be able to take care of herself in crises. She can handle just about any setback life throws her way, such as an illness or death in the family. She thrives intellectually because she is interested in learning new things and in doing the work necessary to keep up in school. She thrives physically because she has the right food and exercise and amount of rest she needs to feel well. And, she thrives spiritually because she knows she can believe in the goodness she has always found modeled by her family.

Signs That a Home Is Preventing a Child's Growth

Homes that model pessimism and negative expectations on a fairly constant basis tend to reinforce a child's inadequacies, rather than his strengths. The child may be told that his attempts to do anything don't work and cannot work because he doesn't have what it takes. The child's accomplishments may be put down as showing off. "You're just trying to show you're better than other people in this family," is the kind of thing said in some families when a child achieves something worthy of attention.

Or the child's feelings of success may be undermined. "Don't get a swelled head about these grades. You should have gotten them years ago!" one mother told her high school daughter who learned how to buckle down and study in her senior year.

Negativism in families does not necessarily mean the family may be unhappy. But it can keep children in the family from accomplishing—or feeling good about accomplishing—the tasks necessary to go from one life stage to another. It can also make the children unhappy, tense, angry, and aggressive. As one thirty-seven-year-old man described growing up in his negatively charged home, "I was ready for verbal combat all the time. I was always fortifying my mind with comebacks I could use the next time my parents or brothers said something mean to me. By the time I was nine or ten, I was responding to every remark with bitter sarcasm." This man has not progressed well through the stages of life. His combative, sarcastic personality has kept him from succeeding at his career—he's a high school social studies teacher who gets into disputes with his students and school administrators—and from being able to have satisfying relationships with women he loves.

While such loving fictional heroines as Anne in the *Anne of Green Gables* series and Pollyanna in the *Pollyanna* series succeeded at overcoming others' grumpiness with their cheery personalities, most children give up trying to be nice when their efforts are put down. They begin to believe that pleasantness and optimism are not welcomed in the home and are not going to help anyone get what he wants in life—unless they are used as tools to manipulate.

There are other methods of hindering a child's intellectual, spiritual, physical, and emotional growth besides use of put-downs, insults, and devaluing comments. One of the most damaging of these methods is idolizing a child. When parents and other family members idolize and idealize a child too much, they might be protecting her from having realistic perceptions about herself and her real-life limitations. This child's talents could be so inflated by adoring parents that the child is devastated when she finds she can't be better at everything than everyone else. The child is protected from having to be accountable for anything in life—grades, jobs, even self-care. She will have a hard time progressing through the stages in life because she hasn't learned how to be responsible for herself.

Another problem with child-worshipping families is that they tend to play favorites—often coddling one child and denigrating another child in the family. Or parents can display these different approaches to the same child, changing from negative to overpositive behaviors in the bat of an eye for no apparent reason. This kind of sudden change, however, is often caused by mental illness—a topic that needs a special section of its own.

....
Mental Illness Examined

Some parents who perpetuate negativism in the home do so because of mental illness in the family. The behaviors of mental illness can be passed down in families for generations genetically, through modeling, or both.

It is very possible for a mentally ill parent to be undiagnosed. This parent can spend her adult years believing her actions and feelings are triggered by the behaviors and attitudes of her children and others in the family. Often, these children and sometimes the other parent believe they really are to blame for this parent's moods and behaviors, and they suffer all kinds of guilt as well as fear, anger, and despair, among other unwanted emotions.

Any of the following behaviors can be a sign of mental illness severe enough to be considered psychosis. These symptoms are adapted from the *Diagnostic and Statistical Manual of Mental Disorders, Fourth Edition,* more commonly known in the mental health field as the *DSM-IV.*

- Depression so severe it renders the victim unable to want to do anything positive, let alone try to do anything positive, for anyone, including himself.
- Mood swings that include periods of almost wild euphoria characterized by such impulsive acts as taking extravagant vacations, moving to a new city, and making grand plans for starting businesses, followed by periods of despair so deep they cancel out all plans of the euphoric period.
- The hearing of voices and seeing of hallucinations that can seem to be coming from some outside source such as demons, angels, or ghosts.
- The belief that everyone—including every family member—is either part of some evil conspiracy or is in danger of being harmed by people colluding in evil conspiracies.
- The changing of personalities, sometimes in the middle of a conversation. From a no-nonsense adult, this person can suddenly switch to a giddy, childlike flirt, or from a loving mom or dad to a tough-minded, impatient tyrant. These changes may be so subtle they are almost impossible to perceive, or they may be

obvious enough to others in the family to keep them in a constant state of confusion. Just when these family members think they know this person, that person's personality shifts again. This person can have separate lives, one of which is that of a responsible parent, while the other might be one of risk taking and thrill seeking with an entirely different social set. The possibilities are endless. Sometimes the personalities are aware of the others (there can be many personalities living in the same person), sometimes not.

- The inability to recover from a traumatic event. In her work as a therapist, Audrey deals with this condition on a regular basis. It's called post-traumatic stress disorder in *DSM-IV,* is more commonly referred to as PTSD, and can happen to anyone at any time in life. Symptoms include the inability to regulate weeping; unexpected flashbacks to the traumatic event; a desperate desire to avoid people, places, and objects that remind the victim of the event; and problems with sleeping, concentrating, and remembering. Sometimes the traumatic event will be remembered vividly in flashbacks; other times it will be repressed from memory altogether. A traumatic incident can be anything that disrupts the survivor's life, from an act as violent as a rape or armed robbery to a mild fender bender. Loss of property to natural causes and the death or illness of a loved one can also cause PTSD.

These symptoms of mental illness can vary from mild enough to seem almost normal to so severe the parent is incapacitated or harmful to herself or others. The problem for family members is admitting that the behaviors might really be indicative of true mental illness—which is sometimes very hard to do. It's much easier to attribute these behaviors to the parent's nature ("She's just high strung"), hard life experiences ("He was abused and abandoned in childhood"), or treatment by other family members ("None of the other kids or my dad shows her the respect she needs"). But it's most helpful for family members to avoid such rationalizations and instead seek help, as treatment for mental illness is accessible and effective. Today's medications are so effective, in fact, that many people diagnosed with mental illness can enjoy normal lives.

Less severe mental conditions that do not indicate psychosis but still affect family well-being are considered personality disorders. All those described in *DSM-IV* could be damaging to family happiness, but three bear particular mention: narcissistic, antisocial, and dependent personality disorders.

The parent with a narcissistic personality disorder believes, and acts as though he believes, that the family exists for him and revolves around him, and that family members have no needs, thoughts, or feelings of their own. Any attempt to suggest otherwise could produce great rage and accusations of being selfish and never thinking of others.

The parent with the antisocial personality disorder may keep the family withdrawn from the world, secluded from friends and outside family members. Any attempts of children to have a social life outside the home may be denounced as showing disloyalty.

The parent with the dependent personality disorder might see any attempt of a child to grow and develop a life outside the home as abandoning her and removing a crucial source of support. The child may grow up believing that his only choices are cleaving to the parent for life or leaving that parent to a terrible, lonely fate.

As with the symptoms of psychosis, these symptoms of personality disorders can range from mild enough to be considered eccentric to severe enough to cause dread and depression in everyone in the home. They can be treated successfully with medication and psychotherapy. Without treatment, personality disorder symptoms that are mild and occur infrequently can escalate over time into symptoms that are chronic and severe.

Whether the parent with mental illness or personality disorder goes into treatment, other family members should seek help through individual therapy, support groups, or both. A local helpline should be able to provide a choice of affordable treatment facilities. A good source of information on mental illness in families is the National Alliance for the Mentally Ill (NAMI), which can be contacted via its Web site, www.nami.org. Try the phone book, also—there might be a local chapter of NAMI in your town. Besides providing lots of information, NAMI representatives will advise you on getting help and will be a source of comfort and support.

Parents who are not mentally ill and who try practicing the Six Steps will become aware of ways in which they promote or impede their children's growth through the stages of life. They will recognize their own negativism or coddling in the way they relate to their kids. They'll be able to figure out what the kids need from them in order to keep on growing into the independent, happy people nature intended them to be.

We encourage families to consider the Six Steps as heirlooms. You may not be able to pass down a complete set of Harvard classics or pieces of Waterford crystal because those heirlooms aren't in your family. But everyone can give the much more valuable gifts of modeling; consistency; reinforcement; rational empathy; caring for pets, plants, and things in the children's lives; and caring for the children and for all the people in their lives. These heirlooms cost no money at all and will continue to improve lives from one generation to the next.

Now, on to chapter 10, "How to Implement the Six Steps Every Day, All Day." There are several ways to incorporate the Six Step Plan into your life. This chapter describes seven easy and enjoyable ways to do so. You can try them all and decide which ones you like best.

chapter 10

•••••• ▣ ••••••

How to Implement the Six Steps Every Day, All Day

This chapter describes seven enjoyable ways to incorporate the Six Step Plan into your life. Some of them are easier than others. Pick the one that suits your style, or try them all until you decide which one you like best.

••••••••••••••••••••••••
The Chart Method

On a piece of poster paper at least fourteen inches wide by twenty-four inches long, create a grid consisting of two-inch squares, with seven squares across the top and twelve running down the side, so you can list the steps you use more than once. You'll need a new chart every week. The larger your chart, the more room you will have to record your use of a step.

At the top, list the days of the week. Every time you find yourself using a step, record it on a square. You can use the initials M (for modeling), R (for reinforcement), RE (for showing rational empathy), CPT (for caring for plants, pets, and things), and CP (for caring for people). Use "Con-M, Con-R, Con-RE, Con-CPT, and Con-CP every time you are consistent in using a step.

We suggest keeping the chart on a desk or table for easy

access. If you want a smaller chart, use a separate sheet of paper for every day of the week.

At the end of every day, you can see by the number of entries how well you have used the Six Step Plan, and you can then challenge yourself to improve your record the next day.

The Workbook Method

Buy a three-ring binder and six divider sheets. Fill the binder with at least 120 sheets of loose-leaf paper, either lined or unlined, placing twenty pages in each section. Or, buy a notebook that has six dividers. Label each divider with the name of a step. This will be your "workbook." Keep this workbook in the place nearest your "writing" chair. If that's in the kitchen, you might store the workbook on a shelf or in the cabinet where you keep your recipe books. If your writing place is in your snuggling chair in your bedroom or living room, store the workbook in a nearby drawer. If your writing place is in your car, where you wait for children to finish sports practice or lessons, keep the workbook in your glove compartment.

If you can only find time to write while you're in waiting rooms or on buses or trains, keep the workbook in your purse or briefcase—you'll have to buy a notebook that's small enough to fit.

YOUR NEW BEST FRIEND

Regard your workbook as your new best friend, always there to hear you out, to let you ventilate, and most of all, to keep track of your progress.

Mark each divider with one of the Six Steps. Record your progress in this workbook at least once a day. Put the date at the top of each page, followed by a list of the family problems you dealt with.

Here are some sample entries to get you started with your own. Let yourself enjoy this journal keeping—think of it as writing a book about your family life as that life actually takes place.

On a modeling page, you might write something like the following entry: "July 18, Susie's bad grades in math, the boys' fighting, and Jane's sulking because she can't take guitar lessons. Bobby's temper tantrums, all the kids' bickering about food, not feeding the hamsters," and so on. Now just list all the ways you used the modeling step for dealing with each situation. Or, write about how you could have used it to your advantage.

For instance: "When I came in from work, the boys were arguing loudly over something one of them said. They were just going at each other. I modeled cheerfulness and ignored the arguing. I gave each one of them hugs and said I was glad to see them and said something nice about each one of them—that Tom's hair looked great and Bobby's chest was getting bigger.

"Susie came in and yelled about getting another D in algebra. I modeled empathy by saying she must have felt bad about that when she saw her paper, and I'd be glad to help her find a tutor when she was ready for one.

"I modeled caring for Jane by giving her a big hug despite the fact she was sulking and didn't hug me back. I modeled loving care of pets by feeding the hamsters, whose food and water dishes were empty, talking to the hamsters in loving tones so the kids would know I was caring for the pets.

"Then I went in the kitchen and began cutting up veggies for a giant salad, feeling my whole body relax as I worked with the food. As the kids wandered in, I modeled love of the food preparation by telling them how much I love working with the beautiful vegetables and giving them slices of red and yellow peppers to eat. Jane and Bobby complained they missed their Tater Tots, and I just smiled and acknowledged that our new way of eating would take time to get used to. 'Here, try some carrot dipped in olive oil—mmm.' Of course they refused, so I ate the carrot and modeled thorough enjoyment of it.

"Susie eventually began watching me cut and slice and toss and asked what the different veggies were. Then she said she wanted to cut the parsley up because 'it's all green and fluffy.' Success!

"At dinner, I modeled pleasure in eating the salad and modeled empathy with those kids who said they hated it. I said, 'I know healthy food is hard to get to like; it's so different from what you're used to.' And I smiled, smiled, smiled.

"I think I like modeling because it lets me show the kids what I enjoy and not have to worry if they don't enjoy it, too. I know they eventually will probably enjoy what I enjoy if I continue the modeling with consistency because that's how modeling works.

"The hardest part of modeling is ignoring the bad stuff that's happening with the kids when I want to model a loving and cheerful disposition. It's hard to keep the focus on that cheeriness instead of letting the bad stuff, the fighting and complaining, get me down. But in the end, it's better for me because it doesn't sap my energy and goodwill. I just keep telling myself that I can have a cheerful atmosphere in my home and the source of it can be me."

Other entries might include, "Did not give in to Jane's insistence that I make her some fried eggs because she hated the salmon" on the consistency page. Or "Served the healthy food with gorgeous garnishes of red and yellow peppers, making sure all of it was organic" on the caring for people page. We hope these sample entries illustrate that there's no right or wrong way to use the steps or to write about using them.

If you don't want to list the problems you're struggling

with ahead of time, just list those problems as they come up, one at a time.

The purpose of the workbook is to show you your problem areas with your family, your most and least successful strategies for dealing with those problems, and your progress in changing the mood of your home. It also keeps you conscious of the need to use the steps daily.

The Diary/Journal Method

This method is similar to the workbook method but is unstructured. It involves writing what you want, using up one page after another. When one book is filled up, you can start another.

Buy some kind of book with blank pages, anything from a spiral notebook to a stylish hardcover book with blank pages, and keep a journal of the ways you use the Six Step Plan. Write as much or as little as you want or as you can when you have time.

Suppose your daughter is getting failing grades in two or more of her subjects. You would list the date and then describe all the ways you applied the Six Steps to this grading problem and how they worked.

For one day's entry, you might write, "I am upset at the way Karen doesn't seem to care about her grades. Today I modeled my feelings about grades by saying to her that in our family, kids are expected to get good grades. In our house, we make grades a priority.

"I reinforced her behavior the one time I saw her studying today by bringing her a dish of apples and telling everyone else to leave her alone and letting her know she was very self-disciplined, studying on her own initiative.

"I showed rational empathy by telling her I know it must be hard finding energy to study with her soccer schedule and by giving her some reasons why she has to make Spanish a priority, such as, if she doesn't keep up with her Spanish every day, she'll get behind, and then she'll have to quit soccer and all her other activities until she catches up.

"I showed care for her things by sharpening all her pencils.

"And I showed care for her by calling the high school counselor and asking him to send over a Spanish tutor from the high school.

"The consistency I showed was keeping my temper when Karen told me her grades were her business and not mine. I didn't let myself get pulled into an argument by that remark but just ignored it. That's what my friend Sarah told me she learned from her parenting classes—just ignore things your kids say that are designed to start arguments.

"I think I might take parenting classes next month myself. They certainly did Sarah lots of good; she's so calm with her kids now compared to me. Taking parenting classes would be another way of showing caring, not just for Karen but for the rest of my family."

....
The Discussion Method

For this method, you need to get at least one other parent to meet with you once a week or more for about an hour so you can discuss the ways you implemented the Six Steps with your families. Here are suggested ground rules for these discussions:

1. Have someone volunteer to act as moderator. The moderator is supposed to act as a kind but firm leader of the group, gently enforcing the rules so the discussion does not go off on tangents or turn into an argument.

2. Everybody gets a turn to speak. Discuss any step you want when it's your turn to speak. For five minutes, talk about it and how you applied it. The other people present then give their feedback on how you applied that step and describe how they would have handled it.

3. Limit feedback to five minutes. This rule is important because it helps prevent rambling and provides the opportunity for more discussion from more people.

4. Have one general topic per meeting, such as, "Is Being Tough with Kids Showing Consistency or Inflexibility?" or "The Frustration of Caring for Others When Others Won't Care for Themselves." The topic can be chosen by the moderator. Allow fifteen minutes for free-form discussion of the topic.

5. Set a strict time limit for the meeting. Two hours should be the maximum time allowed. This group can be considered the same as a book group or a parenting support group.

The Mind-Set Method

Read this book at least twice to get the Six Steps embedded in your mind. In the morning, set your mind on implementing the steps during the day. At night, review in your mind how you applied the steps that day. During the day, focus on one step or another as needed. Soon, use of the mind-set method will make use of the Six Steps automatic for you.

The Positive-Thinking Method

When all around you are losing their heads, to paraphrase the famous old poem "If," by Rudyard Kipling, you can draw on the Six Steps to calm everyone down, including yourself, and turn the mood of your home from seething to sweet.

Say, for instance, that full-scale warfare has erupted in your living room because you have stopped paying the cable TV bill. Children are yelling at one another and you, the dog is barking in that vicious way he uses when people argue, and your children's friends are rolling their eyes and saying they are going home.

Instead of yelling back, apologizing, or caving in ("All right, all right, just settle down; I'll have the cable turned back on right now!"), you model. You smile, pick up a book, and begin reading. You reinforce the one child who's not complaining and maybe doing homework: "Joyce, I like the way you're finding something else to do besides watching TV."

You show rational empathy. "Kids, I know you are so used to having all this stuff available on television. But I want to spend the money we spent on cable on sports fees and other expenses."

You show caring for the kids' things: "I want you guys to have new soccer socks this month. Your old ones have holes. There's no way I can afford new soccer socks and the cable bill."

You show caring for the kids themselves: "Soccer is good for you," you say. Then you give another positive smile and model the act of reading a book.

Gradually, the negative behaviors will die down and the negative energy will dissipate as your kids find things to do other than watch TV. The child who was reading will probably come over and give you a hug. The dog will probably come over for a pet. The scene will be much sweeter than it was, something the other kids will appreciate even if they don't ever tell you so.

The Reminder Method

Write, draw, use calligraphy, or cross-stitch the Six Steps on separate pieces of paper or canvas or cardboard. Frame every one of them in frames of your choice. Hang them around your house where you are likely to see them. Or, if you're less artistically inclined, write them on self-stick notes and put them on furniture, the refrigerator, walls, the car dashboard, wherever you want. The next time you are tempted to scream at a child, nag your spouse, feel sorry for yourself, send out for greasy pizza you can't afford, let the fern go unwatered, tell a child to lie about his age at the movie theater so he can get in for less, or do anything else you don't want your family members to do, you can glance at a step reminder and stop yourself short.

You'll think of other ways to incorporate the Big Six into your life—ways that work best for you.

Now, on to chapter 11, "Case Histories: Unhappy Homes." Case histories are effective ways of illustrating why and how situations happen. The case histories in chapter 11 will help you understand why and how homes turn unhappy. This chapter will examine a variety of unhappy homes, from those where people are blatantly unhappy to those where unhappiness hovers beneath a veneer of pleasantness.

chapter 11

Case Histories:
Unhappy Homes

The parents in the following stories meant well and were good parents in many ways. It's just that their own ambitions took precedence over the well-being of other family members. You'll see at the end of these case histories how the painful damage inflicted by these parents' ambitions could have been avoided if these parents had been using the Six Step Plan.

The Jones Family

Eugenia and Norman Jones are teachers and have been heads of their high school departments—English for Eugenia and science for Norman—for more than twenty years.

Eugenia and Norman have sixteen-year-old twin daughters named for their grandmothers, Ethel and Molly. Ethel makes her parents very happy. She is pretty, she is popular, she keeps her nails manicured, she gets good grades, she does well in track and soccer, she has a nice boyfriend, and she is pleasant to have around.

Molly is like a pale copy of Ethel. She tries to look and act like Ethel but never quite succeeds.

Since they were young, the girls have been given two sets

of messages. Ethel, who is naturally outgoing and bright in school, has been told she is terrific and is indeed successful. Molly, who has a serious, questioning nature and is not as quick to learn in school, has been told she is depressing and no fun to be around. Molly has also been told she is needy for attention, a trait that annoys her mother to no end.

As Ethel thrived and Molly lagged behind, the girls turned these messages into reality. Molly is blamed for not doing better in life. She is told that she always knew she had personality problems to overcome and would have to try harder. If she was not able to overcome her personality problems (mainly shyness and awkwardness around other people), it was because she didn't try hard enough. In other words, she has only herself to blame.

Molly is trying harder, but nothing she does is working. She is taking Ritalin in an attempt to focus better in class, be more animated with people, and improve her grades. She is trying yet another sport, racquetball, and making a real effort to smile more and be more outgoing. These efforts are made easier with the Ritalin, but her actions come across as artificial. Molly's one friend, Sally, tells her that she's just not herself on Ritalin, and Molly feels Sally is right. But she also feels that her natural personality is so blah that she has to take Ritalin.

Eugenia and Norman Jones and their daughters believe that their family is happy. Three out of four of them are happy, and the fourth would be happy, too, if she could just "make up her mind to fit in better," as her parents put it (they believe her problems are due to her lack of willpower). They think Molly should realize how lucky she is to be part of such a neat family and try harder to be like the rest of them.

The truth is, no family is ever really happy if one member is made to feel bad about him- or herself. Every member of a family is as important as every other member of the family and deserves to feel that way. What Norman and Eugenia are modeling is rejection of a daughter, with alarming consistency. They let Molly know she's never going to be considered acceptable to them—and get the unqualified love from them that Ethel is given—unless she is able to measure up to their standards.

They reinforce Molly's sense of failure by favoring Ethel in obvious ways. When the family is together, Ethel is treated like the perennial guest of honor, while Molly's comments and attempts to be a part of the conversations are treated as unwelcome intrusions—either ignored or acknowledged with impatient glances.

Molly doesn't express anger at her family for treating her poorly; she just keeps hoping that someday she'll measure up enough to get the same treatment Ethel gets. Eugenia and Norman do not provide Molly with rational empathy. Instead, they tell her she should feel bad about her poor grades and lack of popularity in school. If she didn't feel bad about these things, Eugenia and Norman reason, why would she ever be motivated to improve?

These parents show care for their house, their plants, and their pet Corgi, because these things please them. They help Ethel with her car and her care of her clothes, because Ethel is doing so well in ways that please them. But they do not help Molly with her clothes because, they tell her all the time, she doesn't take care of them. She does not hang her clothes up properly, keep her hems hemmed, or keep any clothes well pressed. Her parents are always criticizing her clothing as well as her hair (which is never clean or neat enough for them). And Molly has been told that with grades so low, she can forget about being given her own car.

As for caring for the people in the home, the parents give Molly and Ethel the same kind of medical and dental care. Molly gets counseling sessions with a nurse-practitioner friend of her parents who prescribes her Ritalin. This nurse-practitioner is not a therapist but is a "good listener." Eugenia herself determined that this nurse-practitioner should prescribe the Ritalin Molly takes because she read about its behavior-modifying benefits in parenting magazines.

Molly's school counselor has advised Eugenia and Norman to have Molly assessed by a psychiatrist for depression, but the parents believe they can tell better than a stranger whether their daughter is depressed.

Sometimes, Molly tells her school counselor, it seems as if her parents and her sister are able to be as happy as they are because they can look down on her. She is probably right. Many families create a scapegoat child in order to have a sense of solidarity and cohesion among the other family members. Dave Pelzer's memoir, *A Child Called "It,"* is a devastating example of this family dynamic carried to extremes.

··························
The Milano Family

Myrna married Umberto Milano, a handsome, loving gentleman whose favorite spare-time activities are preparing huge Mediterranean meals for his family and sculpting. He has always been satisfied with his career as a massage therapist and devoted to his many regular clients.

In contrast to Umberto, Myrna's father, brother, and two uncles are wiry, energetic, ambitious men whose spare-time activities include running marathons and attending medical conferences all over the world. They put a lot of emphasis on trying to improve their careers as medical doctors in their respective specialties.

Umberto has a special reason for devoting his efforts to his clients and his family. His family in Italy had never forgiven him for marrying a woman who was not Italian or Catholic. So, after meeting and falling in love with Myrna when she was an exchange student in Florence, Umberto came to America with her determined to make her country his own. His efforts to reconnect with his Italian family failed. His Italian family blamed his running off with Myrna for causing his mother's heart attack—yet another reason why he is unable to connect with his family back in the country where he was raised.

The marriage of Myrna and Umberto was very happy at first. Umberto learned massage therapy as a means of earning an income while going through medical school. But upon realizing he loved massage work and the benefits it brought to his clients, he dropped out of medical school.

Still wildly in love with her husband, Myrna said she didn't care what he did for a living—just as long as they were together.

But when she and Umberto would visit with her parents and siblings and see how much status and income they had, she would feel uneasy and dissatisfied.

Myrna and Umberto had two children—Loring, named for Myrna's father, and Lora, also named for her father. Early on, Lora showed a preference for art and music and literature and watching her father, Umberto, at his work. She would practice giving her dolls massages from the time she was three years old.

Loring, however, was a prodigy in math and science and so was groomed for the medical field from the time he was in kindergarten—a prestigious kindergarten that took only one out of every three hundred applicants. Myrna was determined that he become as successful a physician as her father. She then began devoting most of her energies to Loring's development—tutoring him in his schoolwork, having him take music lessons to enhance his cognitive functioning, getting him on waiting lists for the right elementary and high schools, and lining up the right tutors for his SAT exams several years ahead of time. The money required for these schools was supplied willingly by Myrna's father.

Lora was left to develop on her own. She became a naturally kind and loving person with an interest in Reiki.

Umberto had begun to feel estranged from Myrna's family after about five years of marriage. He told Myrna that Loring was the only one in their family who Myrna's parents—and for that matter, Myrna herself—seemed to care about.

Myrna did not actually disagree. She had by then realized that her husband and daughter would not fulfill her financial and social ambitions. She had decided she was right to devote most of her time and energy to the development of her son. She did not deny Umberto's sad observation that she spent almost no time with him anymore and that her passion for him had clearly waned.

But when Myrna and Umberto began discussing divorce, her passion for him did return, unexpectedly. After a romantic trip to the Bahamas, Myrna decided she didn't want to let Umberto go. She promised she would try harder to be the kind of devoted wife her husband deserved. Umberto was ecstatic because he had never stopped loving her, and he hoped that the happiness of their first few years of marriage would return.

For a few months, Myrna fulfilled her promise to be a more devoted wife. But, gradually, she went back to her own activities. This couple became ever more estranged again as Myrna devoted more and more of her spare time to an unpaid but very time-consuming career as a medical organization volunteer. She raised money for hospitals, volunteered in hospital gift shops, and obtained a position on a hospital's board of directors. She hosted teas, luncheons, and dinners for hospital auxiliary organizations.

When the children were in high school, Myrna tried to persuade Umberto to return to medical school and become an osteopath so he could use his hands-on skills to better advantage. But she gave up when she realized that, however good a massage therapist Umberto might be, he was just not medical school material.

This failure of her efforts to "improve" Umberto's career status caused Myrna to become ever closer to her son. She made sure Loring took the right math and science courses needed to get into the right medical school. She supervised his spare-time activities down to the minute, knowing that volunteering in the right organizations was just as important to medical school admissions committees as getting the right grades in the right courses.

Loring did gain admission to a college with a satisfactory premed program. But the constant pressure from his mother to allow her to run his life caused Loring to become depressed. He began to self-medicate with marijuana and alcohol and let his class assignments slide.

By the middle of spring semester in his freshman year, Loring was refusing to return his mother's calls or let her in when she tried to visit.

Finding his mother waiting in his dorm room when he returned from an all-night party one morning, Loring turned around, left the room, and kept going till he had reached the apartment of a friend off campus. There he stayed, selling drugs for the friend to earn his rent and abusing alcohol and drugs.

About six months later, Loring finally got treatment for his drug abuse, entered a rehabilitation program, and is now living in a group home, where he has therapy several times a day. His parents and sister are in family therapy, too, but Myrna misses most of the sessions because of her commitments to her various hospital organization activities. She dealt with her disappointment in her son by throwing herself even more into her hospital volunteer work.

Lora assists Umberto in his massage-therapy practice and attends a charter high school that emphasizes fine arts.

Is anyone in this family happy? That's hard to say. Except for Lora and Umberto, who are close, there isn't any family anymore, at least not in the cohesive sense of the word. That's because Myrna has never shown real caring for the people in her family, at least not as they are. The only reason she cared for her son, Loring, was because he showed the potential to do what she wanted him to do: become as successful as her father.

Myrna has not shown much of any respect, let alone caring, for her daughter's interests in life, such as the arts of Reiki and other forms of energy healing.

Myrna also has shown little empathy for Umberto or Lora. If she would try to understand their feelings, she might understand how estranged from her she has caused them to feel. They also feel abandoned and disdained. Nor has Myrna shown real empathy for her son—she has only cared that he was meeting her goals for him, not how he might be feeling about those goals—or his own life.

But Myrna may have lost touch with her ability to feel empathy. When Umberto told her in a family therapy session how out of place he felt with her parents and brothers, how inferior and looked down upon, Myrna could not feel his pain. She told him frankly that if he wasn't going to achieve more in life, he had to get used to feeling out of place with people who were more successful than he.

As for modeling, Myrna models disregard, impatience, and rejection with her husband and daughter. She modeled smothering possessiveness with her son and would probably still do so if he were still in college and following her plans for his life.

The only behaviors in her family that Myrna reinforced

were the study habits shown by Loring before he became depressed.

It is probably Lora's good fortune that Myrna left her alone to develop on her own. Due to the fact that Umberto used all Six Steps in his relationship with his daughter, Lora is now a relatively happy and fully actualized young woman.

Umberto would have used the Six Steps with Loring, too. But Myrna took control of raising their son.

The O'Flaherty Family

Sean and Maureen O'Flaherty married when they were both twenty-one, and they eventually had four children, one boy and three girls. Sean felt mostly overwhelmed with fatherhood and the frequent layoffs he encountered in the construction field. He often thought of moving to a place where work was more plentiful, but he didn't want to uproot the children from their schools.

Maureen, a pretty woman who attracted lots of male attention, was impatient with the penny-pinching. She thought she could do a lot better for her children if she found a man who was more affluent.

So, when the children were ages ten to seventeen, Maureen moved out and began her search for a new husband. She thought the children would make it difficult for her to present the image she needed to find the kind of new mate she wanted.

The children begged their mother not to leave, but to no avail. She told them it was for the best and that in a year or so they'd be glad because she could offer them a lot more in life.

Sean, the father, did his best to care for the children, but it was difficult. At times they'd run into Maureen and her prospective new husbands at various places in town. She would wave at them, sometimes stop and ask how they were, and then just turn away. Unable to be both mother and father to his children, Sean let the house get messy and the kids more or less bring up themselves.

Sure enough, within a year and a half, Maureen had remarried a widowed businessman. They bought a large house, and Maureen began having her children come over more and more often, staying longer and longer until, finally, three of them were living with her and her new husband.

The youngest daughter, Nula, refused to reunite with her mother. She had missed her mother so much when her mother left the family, and had become so disillusioned with her father's inability to care for his children properly, that she had vowed never to need any family member again. She moved to Hollywood and became a successful actress. Once, in an attempt to reconcile with her mother, she invited her mother to visit her and her fiancé in their new home. But Maureen saw that the fiancé was high on cocaine most of the time she was visiting and told Nula not to marry him. Nula was furious with her mother for giving her this warning and said her mother had not earned the right to tell her what to do. She vowed never to speak to her mother again and has remained firm in that commitment.

Nula's husband did prove to be addicted to drugs at that time, and Nula divorced him after their daughter was born, some five years later. Today, Nula's mother and siblings are together as a family and have a healthy family relationship with Maureen's husband, now their stepfather. Nula's exhusband has gone into treatment and remarried, and Nula is raising her daughter alone.

Nula's career seems to have slowed down. She is no longer in such demand for the ingenue roles she had always played. Her romantic life has also reached a plateau. After a few highly publicized affairs that ended badly and quickly, Nula found she could not make a lasting relationship and is now living unhappily as a single mom. She lives in a practically unfurnished, sterile townhouse she says she has no incentive to make look or feel like a home.

Nula's daughter spends most of the time with Nula's ex-husband these days, playing happily with the twin sons his new wife just gave birth to.

Who needed to use the Six Steps in this family's situation? Certainly, Maureen and Sean. But they both have happy families today—even Sean, who is remarried to a divorcée with four children. Nula has never met her father's new family; she says her father is a stranger to her now.

Nula is the one who could benefit most from the Six Steps. If she would show caring for her original family members, she might find herself forgiving her mother and being able to have the mothering she has missed so much and needs in order to have love in her own life. If she could care more for her home, she could develop the family life with her daughter that both of them need. If she gave rational empathy to her mother and ex-husband, she would explain to her mother how she felt when her mother left her and her siblings with their father. She could explain to her ex-husband how threatening it was for her when he took drugs. She could tell her dad she loves him but fears she would feel like an outsider when she visits because she has learned from his letters to her that his new family is very close-knit. If she could model connecting behavior with her father, her mother, and her ex-husband with consistency—reinforcing their attempts to connect with her with warmth and love—Nula would find her life becoming much happier.

These steps would take great effort on Nula's part, however, because she is still bitter and angry.

What could Nula do? She could process this anger with the help of a therapist. In exploring her own childhood with the therapist, Nula would realize that loving, caring, consistent, and reinforcing behaviors were never modeled for her. In reliving her anger at her mother in therapy, Nula would be able to let go of it and relate to her mother as the person her mother is now, today.

She would be able to see that her mother not only left her when she was a child, but also stayed away from her—exactly the kind of behavior that Nula displays with her mother now. Nula is modeling this staying-away behavior with her own daughter. That is sad because this little girl would probably have a very good time visiting with her grandmother, her grandfather, and their respective families. These insights might help Nula process her anger and heal enough emotionally to be able to reconnect with the mother and other family members she so desperately needs.

These three stories of unhappy families show that the Six Steps, when practiced sincerely, can do the following:

- Let people be themselves, as they are naturally.
- Help people feel good about themselves, as they are.
- Encourage the kind of caring and nurturing that children need.

The case histories in chapter 12, "Case Histories: Happy Homes," will focus on a variety of happy families, including those that may appear to be in crisis—especially financial and emotional crises—a lot of the time.

chapter 12

•••••• ▣ ••••••

Case Histories: Happy Homes

The case histories in this chapter focus on homes with happy families. Each of the Six Steps is identified in these case histories to help you understand how and when the parents are applying them.

••
Nine Children and the Six Steps

Jerry and Jill Myers planned to have only three children. But the accidental fourth pregnancy went well, and Jill realized she was so happy being pregnant (her husband said "she just glowed") that they kept on going until they had nine children—four boys and five girls. They probably would have had more, but Jill's tenth and eleventh pregnancies ended in miscarriages. "We saw every new baby as a gift from God," Jerry said.

Jerry and Jill's story isn't impressive because they have nine kids. It's impressive because they have nine kids and have never brought in more than $12,000 a year, mostly because Jerry takes jobs that allow him as much time off as possible.

While the children were very young, they lived in a three-bedroom house with one and a half bathrooms. The boys had one bedroom and the girls had another. Family treats included a night out once a week for fun. Fun could be anything—going for walks *en famille* in the evening or going to high school sports games, a free museum, or a school program.

Other treats included sitting next to Daddy at dinner—not because Daddy was so beloved, but because "the food always started with me at meals," Jerry said, with a smile.

Television was allowed to be on for special programs chosen by Jerry and Jill, never as a babysitter or as a way to avoid boredom.

But then, the children were almost never bored. They were too busy with chores, family meetings, outside sports and projects, and one another. "With nine children in the house," Jerry said, "there's always someone to play with."

Discipline was easy. Arguments among the kids were allowed to be worked out by the children unless they got to be too loud, in which case a parent would arbitrate. The kids knew that Dad or Mom's word was law.

Chores could be chosen but had to be done. Sunday after church was chore time, when the house was picked up, vacuumed, and dusted; beds were made; and bathrooms scrubbed. Dishwashing was rotated among the kids—Jerry and Jill never had a dishwasher—and Mom did the cooking with rotating assistants.

This schedule was inviolate. "It had to be, or we'd have lived in chaos," Jill said. And all the kids understood this simple fact of life. A sibling who didn't do his or her share was immediately and hotly resented by the others.

School achievement was also the result of peer pressure and support. Because they all went through the same elementary, middle, and high schools, often having the same teachers, the older children told the younger ones how to deal with teachers and helped with homework whenever requested to do so—they had had many of the same homework assignments themselves. Teachers thought highly of the Myers children, Jerry said. That's because the Myers kids were well behaved, willing to learn, and respectful. As a result of their positive experiences in school, four of the children are now math and science teachers in high schools.

All the Myers children were involved in many activities. "We had a huge wall calendar," Jerry recalls. "It literally covered one wall. On it we had the kids' names and the days of the month. Everyone's schedule was listed on the calendar. Every morning we'd have a meeting and decide who was going to drive whom where and pick whom up." The family's main volunteer activity was a nonprofit foundation started by Jerry and a friend in Mexico. "We would give clothes and toys to the poor kids there every time we went down to go fishing. As people in our town heard about this town, they began donating money so we could buy things the Mexican people needed, like diapers." The Myers children would take turns going to Mexico to help distribute the donated items. Today, the program is a flourishing nonprofit organization with doctors, dentists, and nurses donating their time and skills every month.

How did Jerry and Jill manage to spend enough quality time with each child when they had so many children needing their attention? Jerry said he scheduled weekly individual talking sessions. "I would spend alone time with every child at least once a week, during which the child could talk to me about anything. Sometimes these alone times took place during errands in the car. But these individual attention sessions were never postponed; they were a priority and were always carried out, no matter what. I think I got to know my kids a lot better by having these weekly sessions with them."

Jill was available to the children more on an as-needed basis. She found that the time spent preparing meals with a child was often the time when the child would talk about something important to him or her.

Today, only three children are still at home; the rest have gone on to marriage, jobs, and college. But the children who live nearby come back for dinner at least once a week. "And you know what they always do after dinner? They just hang out, reminiscing about the old days and laughing over incidents that meant a lot to them," Jerry said, shaking his head and smiling.

Jerry hastens to add that their family was not always happy all the time. They often worried about money and learned to do without things other families took for granted. But the kids don't seem to remember those problems. "Now we see the kids weren't really affected by those bad times. I guess they got over them all right and have gone on with their lives in good ways."

Without realizing it, Jerry and Jill used the Six Steps in rearing their family. They modeled the kind of behavior valued in this family—cooperation, collaboration, companionship, and commitment—with remarkable consistency. The morning meetings to discuss transportation and the doing of chores after church every week are just two examples of this consistency.

Reinforcement involved letting the children know that they were pulling their weight. Rational empathy was provided by parents during the regularly scheduled alone times but also by siblings on an as-needed basis. Caring for things, pets, and plants was accomplished during chore sessions on Sundays, meal preparation, and other daily activities. Caring for the people in the household was modeled consistently in various ways by everyone in this house.

Unhappy Beginning, Happy Ending

Ellie and Ralph Rocco are an architect and nurse in their early forties who have two daughters, Laurel, sixteen, and Lydia, fourteen. The Roccos are a happy family now, Ellie says, but it hasn't always been that way.

"When Laurel got to be about five years old, she was so controlling she made life miserable for us all," Ellie explained. "This child was defiant, rude, demanding, and manipulative. She charmed teachers and others outside the home. She was just unwilling to be a team player inside the home."

Ellie and Ralph found themselves catering to Laurel's demands and, as a result, straining their relationship. "We were never in agreement on how bad she was at any one time, which caused us to accuse each other of being either too nice to her or too mean to her. I'd think I was the only one who really understood her, and Ralph would think the same thing about himself." The truth was, Ellie said, Laurel was manipulating them both as if they were puppets on a string.

Their other daughter was such a sunny soul, she just let her sister have her way most of the time and made a life for herself outside the home with friends and church activities. "Lydia just let Laurel run roughshod over her—she was dominated by her older sister, and that was hard to watch," Ellie recalls. "I mean it. Laurel would yell at Lydia to pick up clothes that Laurel had left on the floor and to hurry up about it, and Lydia would do it. I think Lydia was just too scared of Laurel to tell her to pick up her own clothes, but then all of us were scared of Laurel."

Finally, Ellie decided to take matters into her own hands. She signed up for a course in parenting she heard about from a friend. This course helped parents deal with strong-willed children who disrupt the balance of the home. Within a few weeks, Ellie found the parenting classes to be a source of hope and help. Ellie stopped getting in terrible arguments with Laurel and stopped giving Laurel all her energy and attention. She began enjoying her husband and other daughter again.

Ralph let Ellie teach him the parenting techniques she was learning and used them himself with Laurel.

After some very angry protesting, Laurel finally realized that her parents were changing. She saw that they weren't going back to their old giving-in style of dealing with her. Little by little, Laurel stopped using willpower as a tool for getting her needs met and started cooperating. She began to find she liked cooperating. Soon, she and her parents became friendly with one another. Today, Laurel and Ellie go on lunch and shopping trips, as do Laurel and Lydia.

In the interview for this book, Ellie was told about the Six Step Plan and asked if she had used the steps in implementing the changes in her family. She nodded thoughtfully and said that, thinking about it, she had used the steps regularly.

Taking the parenting class in the first place was a way of modeling her willingness to try solving the problems Laurel was causing in the family, rather than ignoring or escaping those problems. Ellie demonstrated consistency when she applied what she learned in the classes without letting Laurel talk her out of using the new parenting methods. Ellie reinforced Laurel when Laurel showed changes in her behavior (e.g., when she picked up after herself instead of demanding that Lydia do it) and reinforced Ralph's and Lydia's courage when they stood up to Laurel. Ellie showed rational empathy when she let Lydia and Ralph know she understood how hard it was to deal with Laurel. She showed rational empathy to Laurel by telling her that she knew that changing behavior wasn't easy to do.

Caring for the plants, pets, and things in the home—

something Laurel had always refused to do and Lydia had never really wanted to do on a regular basis—now became a regular part of both daughters' lives.

Caring for the people in the home was shown in Ellie's decision to pursue the parenting classes in the first place. "I can't say the classes were easy and fun, because they weren't. They also were not a quick fix," Ellie said, "but I kept at them because I cared for the well-being of these people I love."

An Expandable Family

Martha, sixty-six, is a family of one. After divorcing her husband sixteen years ago, Martha found herself in a deep depression for about five years. Despite the fact that her husband was an alcoholic who caused her much unhappiness, she was devastated by the loss. Nothing seemed to lift her spirits, neither medication nor therapy nor Twelve Step Al-Anon groups. She missed her husband dreadfully and didn't care that life was now much more calm and regulated for her. Once, three years after the divorce, she asked him to come back to her, but he was already remarried.

Martha's parents had never been especially loving to her, and her brother seldom contacted her. Her children, who lived across the country and were busy with their own lives, told her rather coldly when she called them that she should be glad she was rid of her husband and should get a life. Martha's attempts to visit them and other far-flung relatives on her vacations were met with warmth on the first visit, coolness on the second, and turndowns when she tried to go back a third time. "We're just too busy," these relatives would say, or, "This isn't a good time."

Martha felt she was being shut out of all family contact for good—which did indeed seem to be true.

An embittered friend of Martha's, who was her age and also alone, expressed Martha's fears in ominous words. "Nobody ever wants to see a single older woman—even if they are related," this friend said bluntly. "Get used to it, Martha—it's not going to change. Oh, they'll come when you're on your deathbed and give you a nice funeral, probably—but that's because it'll be an excuse for them all to get together again and see how everybody's doing."

Martha felt like she had no love coming in and no love to give out—a sterile, sad way of life. Her job as a civil servant in the state motor vehicle department was so routine it offered little help to her spiritually and emotionally.

Then one day Martha read an article in the local paper about a woman who did volunteer work with homeless children—teens who had been abandoned by their families for various reasons. Thinking that at least these kids might need her when no one else seemed to, Martha called the agency. Within a month, Martha had a new life. She had become mentor to three teenagers who had been "dumped" by their families, as they put it, and were living in temporary foster homes.

Martha now helps these teens stay in school, get the services they need from social agencies, deal with problems in their temporary foster homes, and look for jobs and permanent living situations. While the agency will not allow Martha to have the teens live in her home, it does encourage her to give them what support they need—meanwhile giving her any support she needs when she runs into problems with the kids. She provides one-on-one friendship for these children whenever they need to know someone cares or have questions about life.

Today, Martha and the children she mentors are like a core family. Martha meets with them individually at least twice a week, and they all get together on holidays for big dinners at Martha's home. Martha takes them to the doctor if necessary, takes them to the dollar movies, takes them shopping for school clothes at thrift stores, and collects samples of vitamins, makeup, shampoo, toothpaste, and conditioner for them from stores and friends and employees at work. While some of the teens have had drug abuse problems—one, for instance, became a crack cocaine addict after his parents moved to Florida without him on his fifteenth birthday—they are now in recovery. If Martha suspects drug or alcohol use has resumed, she alerts her mentors at the agency so that the proper steps can be taken.

Yes, Martha said, her "family" costs her quite a bit of money and time. "But what else was I going to spend money on? Myself? Travel? A new house? What I needed was other people in my life who made me feel I'm part of a family. I have that now, and it's worth every minute and cent." Martha now has lots of adults in her life as well—she's become good friends with many of the employees at the social service agencies she works with. Now she, too, has photos to hang on her office walls and children's achievements to brag about. She finds people are not just interested in her "family"; they are interested in her, too. Taking care of her own needs has given her a positive new energy that makes her attractive to others—much more appealing as a person.

The Six Steps operate in Martha's "family" in the following ways: She models her beliefs and the behaviors she wants when she talks to "her kids." When she provides items they need, she models caring. In the keeping of her commitments to them, she models consistency. She also models an important behavior for these kids when she uses resources such as social service agencies to help her help them.

Martha is consistent in this modeling. She is careful to

reinforce the teens' efforts to help themselves, to do well in school, and to avoid the temptation to take and sell drugs, drink alcohol, or be with people who do.

But Martha is also modeling for herself the belief that *she* can improve her life, not depend on others to do it for her. This kind of self-sufficiency is what makes her attractive to others.

Martha shows rational empathy to her kids all the time. She listens to their problems, gives rational reasons why the problems exist, and explains why some of their strategies for solving the problems—like dropping out of school or moving in with a boyfriend—are not the best ideas. And she gives herself rational empathy when she gets discouraged, tired, or just too worried about her kids to think she's doing anyone any good.

She models care of plants, pets, and things by making sure her own place is cheery, clean, and hospitable for her kids' visits and by caring tenderly for plants and pets these kids want to keep but are unable to care for. (Yes, Martha has discovered, the parents often "dump" the pets along with the teenagers when they leave.)

As for caring for the people in her life, Martha includes herself in this step as lovingly as she does her kids. She knows if she doesn't take good care of herself, she won't be able to go on enjoying her new life. She gets regular medical exams, gets dental care, and sees a therapist once a week because she finds herself still missing her husband desperately from time to time for no apparent reason. She's learning why she got caught in such a destructive marriage for so long, which is a great source of satisfaction for her emotionally and intellectually. And she attends church regularly because the spiritual pleasure is always unexpectedly helpful to her. Caring for her kids is something she does twenty-four hours a day, seven days a week, in ways that are most sustaining to them without making them overly dependent on her.

Chapter 13 is entitled "Rating Your Childhood Home." This chapter will help you understand whether your childhood home was happy. This understanding prevents you from beating yourself up when things go wrong in your home today and helps you accept yourself as you are—two important factors to using all Six Steps successfully in your home.

chapter 13

•••••• ◘ ••••••

Rating Your Childhood Home

What was your childhood home like? Happy? Sad? Quiet? Argumentative? Full of tension? And why should you or anyone else care?

You should care because you are most likely going to recreate that childhood home for your family. Without realizing what we are doing, we reenact what we know, mainly because we draw from our experience. Here is a case that illustrates this syndrome:

Trish's mother always compared her to others. "Your cousin is good at math; why can't you be good at math? Your sister always looks so nice—why can't you at least keep your hair combed?" Trish hated this practice of her mother's and swore she would never do it to her children.

One day Trish found herself in a psychologist's office with her twelve-year-old son, complaining that he refused to do any homework and was failing two courses.

The therapist asked her son if his siblings had the same problem. Trish interrupted the boy's reply with a loud, "No, his sister always does her homework. Why can't he be more like his sister? I tell him that all the time."

On hearing herself, Trish clapped her hand to her mouth. "Oh, I can't believe it," she said. "I'm my mother! I never realized it until just now." Trish suddenly understood that she had been reenacting her mother's treatment of her without even knowing it.

A year of family and individual therapy plus two parenting classes helped Trish break this habit of comparing her family members to people she admired. She learned to parent her son and her other children in ways that help them to develop, and she learned to appreciate their real selves, warts and all.

How happy was your childhood home? You might need to do some in-depth analysis to get at the truth.

So, take this two-part quiz. The first part deals with healthy parental behavior, and the second part deals with unhealthy parental behavior. Why do we include this negative part of the quiz? It's not because we want to depress you. We just want to give you permission to remember things about your childhood home that you may fear are not "proper" or "okay" to recall because doing so makes you feel disloyal or not a good son or daughter to your parents.

Let's start with the positive quiz. Every category is worth ten points in all, so the highest score you can get is sixty. Lower scores will be explained after you finish the quiz and tally your score. If you had more than one parent, base your answers on the parent who was most influential in your life. Answer quickly, without thinking too much.

Modeling:

My parent was always fairly predictable in behavior, appearance, and attitudes.	T or F
My parent was always fairly well groomed.	T or F
My parent was like my friends' parents.	T or F
My parent made sure our home was pleasant to be in.	T or F
My parent seemed to enjoy being a parent.	T or F

Consistency:

My parent almost always did what he or she said he
or she would do.   T or F

My parent could be relied upon for just about
anything.   T or F

My parent was considered reliable by everyone.   T or F

My parent provided a stable routine for me.   T or F

My parent generally finished what he or she started.   T or F

Reinforcement:

My parent told me when I was doing well.   T or F

My parent respectfully let me know when my dress
or behavior needed changing.   T or F

My parent usually made me feel like I was a valuable
member of the family.   T or F

My parent laughed at my jokes.   T or F

My parent sometimes took my side and always wanted
to hear what I had to say when I had problems with
teachers or other adults.   T or F

Showing rational empathy:

My parent often asked what was happening with me
in my life.   T or F

My parent often asked me what was going on with
me and what I was feeling when he or she didn't
like my behavior.   T or F

My parent would explain to me why I couldn't do
or buy certain things or act a certain way.   T or F

My parent usually seemed to know how I was feeling
about something, good or bad.   T or F

Caring for pets, plants, and things in the home:

My parent always made sure the plants, pets, and
things in our house were cared for.   T or F

My parent made sure I knew how to care for things
I owned, including my pets.   T or F
My parent made me write thank-you notes for gifts.   T or F
My parent took pets to the vet if they needed it.   T or F
When I was little, my parent kept my clothes and
my siblings' clothes clean and ironed and
looking nice.   T or F

Caring for all the people in the home:
My parent got me medical and dental work on a
regular basis, before emergencies happened.   T or F
My parent made sure our home was a place I liked
being in.   T or F
My parent made sure I had regular, healthy meals.   T or F
My parent made sure I got enough sleep and exercise. T or F
My parent made sure I did my homework, did my
chores, and in other ways took good care of myself. T or F

Give every T question two points; F questions get no
points. A score of 51 to 60 means you remember having a
healthy childhood home. A score of 41 to 50 means a childhood home with a few problems. A score of 31 to 40 means a
childhood home with a lot of problems. Any score of 21 to 30
means you were probably living in a home that was troubled
but not all the time. A score of 20 or lower suggests you lived
in a home in which you were unhappy and uncared for most
of the time.

Now for the unhealthy home quiz. Again, give your answers quickly, without thinking. This time, we'll start with
Step Six and go backward.

Caring for all the people in the home:
My parent looked thin and trim while the kids were
overweight.   T or F

We almost never had healthy food in our house.   T or F
My parent took at least an hour to look good enough
    to go out of the house.   T or F
My parent didn't care if I went to the doctor or dentist
    for preventive checkups.   T or F
My parent seldom cared about how I was doing
    in school.   T or F
My parent seldom asked me how I felt about anything. T or F
My parent often told me not to be a pest when I
    started a conversation.   T or F

Caring for pets, plants, and things in the home:
My parent seldom kept our house clean or even
    looking nice.   T or F
My parent did not like pets.   T or F
My parent seldom followed through on care of plants. T or F
My parent seldom cared if my toys needed repair. T or F
My parent seldom got me the equipment I needed
    for sports.   T or F

Showing rational empathy:
My parent seldom talked to me about how my life
    was going.   T or F
My parent seldom asked me any questions at all.   T or F
My parent seldom knew what was in my room.   T or F
My parent seldom tried to talk to me before punishing
    me for something.   T or F
My parent seldom explained to me why he or she did
    anything that affected me.   T or F

Reinforcement:
My parent seldom let me know how I was doing in life. T or F
My parent seldom told me anything but what I
    did wrong.   T or F

My parent seemed to care about how I was doing in
a subject or activity that my parent cared about—
nothing else counted. T or F

My parent put a negative spin on the things I did right. T or F

My parent made depressing predictions about how
I was going to end up in life. T or F

Consistency:

My parent seldom had the same mood from one day
to the next. T or F

My parent always made me anxious about what kind
of mood he or she would be in. T or F

My parent would be nice to me and other people in
public, but in private he or she would be mean to
me and say awful things about the people he or
she had just been nice to. T or F

My parent would make me think it was my fault if his
or her mood was bad. T or F

My parent would never (or almost never) follow
through on promises. T or F

Modeling:

The ways that my parent looked and acted
embarrassed me. T or F

My parent behaved too flirtatiously with people. T or F

My parent was always too bossy with people. T or F

My parent was always phony around people. T or F

My parent always looked tired and upset. T or F

Again, give yourself two points for every true answer. A
score of 51 to 60 means your home was probably a very unhappy place most of the time. A score of 41 to 50 means it
was often an unhappy place with some bright times. A score
of 31 to 40 means your home was probably basically pleasant

with interruptions of unhappiness. A score of 11 to 20 means your childhood home was almost always a good place to be in with a few bad moments now and then. Any score of 10 or lower means you might be repressing some bad memories or idealizing your childhood home. Take the test again, with your mind open.

Analyzing Your Scores

In the positive test, mark the steps in which your score was lowest and think about other ways your parent didn't do so well in these areas. Be honest. Yes, you may love that parent—but these are your private thoughts that you are allowed to have in order to better understand yourself. This is not about blaming or judging your parent.

Now go back to the negative test and look at the steps in which your score was highest. Allow yourself to reexperience bad feelings as you remember the bad times. Add other ways in which your parent provided negative examples of the Six Steps.

When you are finished remembering and feeling, you will probably begin to feel some relief, as though you have cleansed yourself of some bad feelings.

If you don't want to handle the feelings by yourself, get some therapy—it can make a world of difference. The resources listed on our Web site (www.happyfamilieshappen.com) tell you how to find helpful psychotherapy that doesn't cost much money, if any at all.

Are you repeating your childhood home in your home now? Here's another quiz that can answer that question for you. This quiz is about you and your feelings. First, answer the questions with "Yes" or "No." Then, if you can, go back, look at the comments you marked "Yes," and write a few sentences about the situations that evoke the behavior described.

1. I sometimes get feelings of "déjà vu" when I'm with my family at home, as though I'm reliving a situation.
2. I sometimes hear myself saying negative things to my children and spouse that my parents said to me, without thinking about it.
3. I sometimes get a feeling that I have to decorate my house in a certain way—the way it was in the house I lived in as a child—even though I don't share my parents' taste in interior decor.
4. I sometimes worry that if my children don't behave in the same ways I was taught to behave as a child, I am not doing my job as a parent.
5. I sometimes find myself getting mad at my spouse for acting like, or not acting like, my parent of the same sex acted when I was a child.
6. I sometimes find myself worrying that my parents are critical of the job I'm doing as a homemaker and parent.
7. I worry more about how my home should be than how I want it to be.

You probably need a break from dredging up memories at this point, so let's return to your present-day family life.

In chapter 14, you'll begin to see how the media, television, films, and video games might be parenting your children as much as you are. You'll learn how to regain your role as primary parent with the use of the Six Steps.

chapter 14

•••••• • ▣ • ••••••

Media Families

Popular media influences our kids. Books, journal articles, and newspaper stories are full of studies showing how television, video games, films, and music can adversely influence children. This chapter will suggest ways that the media can be controlled in the home using the Six Step Plan.

First, though, let us admit what we know is true: Controlling media in children's lives is difficult. Many parents avoid even trying to regulate the kinds of media their kids play, listen to, and watch, preferring to work on other areas of the children's lives (such as friends and grades) that concern them more.

But you may find that you dislike a lot of what TV and video games bring to your kids. You may be uneasy about the commercialism, even on such "safe" channels as Nickelodeon. You worry about what the fast edits on children's shows are doing to attention spans, and you suspect that the violence on even the mildest video games is desensitizing your kids to the pain and suffering of people and other living things. You may also fear that media is addictive to your children, and you deplore the way your kids head for the game station, TV, or CD player while wearing a Walkman or iPod (lots of kids use media devices simultaneously) as soon as they get home from school. And you've never liked how glassy-eyed and totally mesmerized your children become when they watch the TV screen or play video games.

You don't have to ignore this encroaching of media into your children's lives. You can deal with it now by using all the steps of the Six Step Plan.

Modeling

If you are going to use videos or DVDs to keep your children occupied while you get things done or drive, choose those that require intellectual engagement of some sort. A travelogue about a favorite vacation site or a good children's film might work. The idea is to avoid cartoons that have no meaning beyond instant entertainment. The kids will probably protest: "Why can't we watch cartoons in the car like all the other kids?" But don't feel guilty. Allowing entertainment that fails to provide what Gavriel Salomon, Ph.D., calls "mindfulness" can impede children's intellectual growth. A well-known authority on the effects of children's use of television on their intellectual development, Salomon studied the mental effort involved in TV watching compared with reading and found that the cognitive skills developed in reading were not used at all in TV watching. The implications of these findings suggest, Salomon said, that children might be less willing to use their cognitive abilities in later life—much like people who have seldom exercised are less willing to go for a walk when someone urges them to do so. An article in *Scientific American* entitled "Is Television Addicting?" suggests that mindless watching addicts the brain to more mindless watching because of the repetitive flashing visual images. So, having your kids watch shows that engage intellectual skills—discussing, critiquing, learning—is much better for their minds.

If you have to be at work when your children are at home, make sure they have other things to do besides use media. Craft projects, cooking (if your child is old enough to cook unsupervised), after-school programs, and sports are viable alternatives. Model the behaviors you want while you're at work by saying such things as, "I really enjoy being busy and productive on my job. I want you to be able to enjoy being busy and productive, too. Sitting in front of the TV and playing video games are not productive activities." Then you can discuss with the child those activities you do consider productive and get his input, too.

Now, we're not forgetting the value of pure relaxation. Once in a while, it's okay for you and your kids to relax in front of a program you really enjoy so you can all take a break and be entertained. Most kids have busy, even stressful, schedules these days, and they need some healthy entertainment that gives their minds a rest. Just make sure the entertainment is provided as a treat instead of a steady media diet and is appropriate for their age groups.

Declare that no TV or any other form of media can be used until chores and homework are done. This kind of prioritizing of activities is extremely important for children. If not modeled on a consistent basis, this prioritizing will be neglected. Social workers we know say that this lack of prioritizing leads to all kinds of unwanted conditions in families—dropping out of school, failing to keep jobs, and neglecting sanitary conditions of the home, to name just a few. You might allow the use of headphones during chores but not while doing homework. Kids may insist that they study more efficiently to music, but research shows they really do better with complete quiet.

Be sure to model the kind of media use you do and do not want in your home. Don't flop down on the sofa to watch TV after a hard day unless your own chores—cooking, serving dinner, and cleaning up—are finished first. Don't tell other people in your family who have something to say to you that they have to be quiet until the show you are watching is over. Don't watch TV at the same time you are dressing, playing with, or having a conversation with a child—even a tiny baby.

Model the scheduling of TV watching to a certain time period, such as two hours in the early evening. Limit the use of TV and video games to a few hours a week. (Yes, *week*—not *day*.) Then have one television, one computer play station, and one DVD player in your home, kept in a place like an open family room, where you can see your children's use of these devices at all times. Keep the television in a shared living space rather than in a bedroom. We advise against allowing televisions and computers in bedrooms at all—at least not computers hooked up to the Internet. The dangers of children finding predators on the Internet increases more all the time. A recent study said that one in every six children who use the Internet has unknowingly conversed with a predator disguised as a peer.

It could be that none of these changes is possible to make in your home. Your spouse may be a confirmed media addict who refuses to change. You and your family may be living with people who decide how media will be used. You may have adult children or relatives living with you whose media use you are not able to control. But you don't have to give up. You can model behaviors that let you compete successfully with media's powerful hold on your kids. Here are the most important of these behaviors, in our opinion:

Model an interest in what the children are seeing, hearing, and playing. The disconnect between the media used by children and the parents' knowledge of the content is dangerous. It makes children think parents don't want to know, should not be told, or are too uncool to comprehend what they experience in their own TV or film or video game time.

Ask for a retelling of what your kids just watched. "What happened on *Scooby-Doo* today?" is a good way to start. If they don't answer right away, try these prompts: "Did Velma help a lot? She's my favorite character." If you can't remember characters' names, ask: "What's the main character's name again? What did he do today?" This kind of inquiry exercises all kinds of cognitive skills in kids and teaches them that Mom and Dad welcome active discussions about what they have been doing for the past hour in the family room.

Model rational reasons for your desire to control media use. Say you wanted kids so you could enjoy them and get to know them, not so they could be hooked up to the TV, DVD player, and computer games more than they are to you. Tell them you want kids who learn in school, play sports, and know how to keep house, not kids who are only skilled in operating electronic entertainment devices. Say you had kids so you could love them, not just turn them over to advertisers so they could be told what to buy. The truth is, kids love being talked to about anything, no matter how delicate the subject might be.

Say that you want your children to be able to enjoy reading, not just watching and listening. Then model the joy of reading by reading in your spare time and having lots of books around the house. If everyone likes a certain series of books, you could have a read-aloud of the latest book in that series, with different family members taking reading turns every night. Model your love of music—making music, not just listening to it. In her inspiring memoir, *The Ditchdigger's Daughters,* Yvonne S. Thornton, M.D., says that her father bought musical instruments for all six of his daughters when they were children. These girls were told by their dad not to worry that they had never played instruments before and had no idea how to start, but just start playing. Oddly enough, recalls Dr. Thornton, this "just do it" approach worked. After a period of cacophony, the girls' playing got better. At that point, their father decided it was time to hire a music teacher. After a few years, the girls became so adept at playing music together, they began playing in public, for pay. They put themselves through college by playing at college dances all over the East Coast. June Carter Cash remembered in an interview that her parents told her she had to join the family singers even though she had never sung at all and didn't think she could carry a tune. Much to her surprise, she was able to sing in harmony—without any formal lessons.

Try creating a family orchestra or ukulele band—any kind of group as long as it's live. The making of music together creates a delightful bonding between family members. It can create warm and wonderful memories of family life.

You can also organize family sports activities. A recent Tucson newspaper article told how many local families are now building small skateboard parks in their own backyards. These families' kids now stay home more, and the whole family participates in the skateboarding, either as skateboarders or observers.

Find opportunities to model productive, rather than passive, consumption of media. Produce a video documentary for far-flung relatives—have your children figure out the credits, shots, sequencing, and voice-overs. Take artistic photos of your children and pets and their toys to be blown up for the blank wall in the hall. Make oral history CDs of older family members for Christmas gifts. Other ideas can be brainstormed during dinner.

Model courage—the courage to tell your children that sex and violence-laden media shows could make them feel angry and aroused and want to do things that are not smart for kids to do. But if your spouse loves these shows and is glued to the TV from 6:00 to 11:00 P.M. every night, you don't have to sit by idly and helplessly. Your modeling of the courage to discuss the feelings these shows cause will give your kids the courage to reflect on their feelings. People who've learned to reflect on and accept their feelings, no matter how unacceptable, are going to be healthier. They'll be much healthier emotionally than those who repress and deny unwanted feelings of any kind—especially the kind of unwanted and often scary feelings aroused by violent and prurient TV shows.

Don't think that the effects of sex and violence in a TV show are acceptable if the show has a strong moral lesson. Media-effects researchers have discovered that the actual watching of sex and violence is what arouses sexual and aggressive feelings, whether the feelings are attached to strong morals or not.

Consistency

Consistency can be shown in the way you enforce the media rules in your home and in the way you model all the suggestions listed above.

Reinforcement

Kids should be reinforced with your attention when they develop interests and activities having nothing to do with media watching, listening, and playing. "You are really working hard on your stamp collection today, Doug," you can say, sitting down at his table. "Can you tell me a little about this stamp? It has such an interesting design."

Showing Rational Empathy

Tell your children you understand that most kids are hooked up to media all the time. Tell them about your use of media when you were the child's age. (Audrey remembers her entire family being glued to the test pattern for hours when their first TV set was brought into their home.) Give your children rational reasons why they need to do nonmedia activities, such as talk to people (especially family members), read, write, study, play sports, dance, cook, and play with animals. The reasons can be general—"Human beings weren't meant to be wired-up audience members their whole lives"—or specific— "You need to read and write so you can do well in college and develop your brain. You need to cook and play sports so you can look good and be healthy. You need to play with animals so you can relax and have emotional well-being."

Yes, you can say such wordy, nerdy things to kids. They will listen, even if they don't respond and just roll their eyes. And when they grow up, they will remember almost every word ever spoken and the tone in which it was said.

Caring for Pets, Plants, and Things in the Home

Encouraging care of pets, plants, and things is helping kids wean themselves from media. Show caring for media yourself by taking your kids to live concerts and live theater. Value the albums and classic videos you love by cataloguing, dusting, and, especially, pruning your collection.

Caring for All the People in the Home

As this chapter has indicated, showing care of all the people in the home all the time is crucial for winning the battle with media producers for your children's attention, allegiance, and, yes, love. By talking to your kids in the ways indicated in this chapter, you will be caring for your kids in ways that media cannot.

Your kids may not accept this kind of "talking" care at first. They may even reject it and sneer at it—at first. That's because your kids, along with almost all kids in our culture today, are such passive recipients of the images and characters they see in films, on TV, and in video games that many of them don't feel comfortable having verbal exchanges with adults.

But take heart. Kids will respond to your caring eventually—they want to reattach to their parents and subconsciously miss interacting with them very much.

The conclusion to this chapter is not, as you might expect, that specific or even that hopeful. The media is such a powerful influence on kids today that it can't be mitigated entirely—at least not in homes where both parents have to work, can't and don't want to do homeschooling, and can't handpick their children's friends.

Some media producers adore children and want to enrich their lives in healthy ways. Linda Ellerbee (producer of *Nick News* for the Nickelodeon channel), Jim Henson (the late and much-missed producer of *The Muppet Show*), and of course the producers of PBS children's shows are just a few who care what kids watch. But many media producers try hard to make parents seem not just uncool but dumb. Try watching the thirty or so commercials in an hour of kids' Saturday-morning TV programming if you don't believe us. A determined use of the Six Steps in all aspects of the family's life will create a kind of levee around the family that the media's influence can't get past. And we can say, from our research and experience, that the talking, caring, interested parent is still more necessary for children's development into caring, interested adults than the coolest prepackaged media products sold.

chapter 15

•••••• • ▣ • ••••••

Princes and Prima Donnas: Using the Six Steps to Deal with the Self-Centered Child

Jenise is the mother of two soccer players, a boy and a girl. She and her husband, who live in Phoenix, are devoted soccer parents, taking their children to tournaments all over the state. Recently, the family went to a tournament in Tucson, which is sixty miles from Phoenix. When they arrived, Jenise realized she had forgotten some special equipment. The other soccer parents told her not to worry about it; they could loan the children the equipment they needed. But the children and Jenise's husband were so furious with her for forgetting the equipment that Jenise could not live with her shame. "I turned right around and drove back to Phoenix, doing ninety miles an hour all the way." She was back in Tucson within three and a half hours with the proper equipment. Never mind that the kids only had a half hour or so left to play.

How did Jenise feel, burning up I-10 between Phoenix and Tucson instead of enjoying this long-anticipated tournament? "Bad, of course," she said. "But I knew I had only myself to blame."

This is a family that not only has created but also caters to self-centered kids. These children know they are the centers of their parents' universe because they have been led to believe they are. They are not alone—many American kids today see themselves as the centers of parents' lives.

A recent column by Dave Barry dwelt on the way his four-year-old daughter refused to go to school because his wife was away and he had to do her hair. He had given up choosing outfits because this little girl went into despair if the ensemble she wore didn't go together just right.

A friend's granddaughter, who had just turned five, had a shrieking tantrum the last time our friend visited because her parents wanted to go straight out to dinner at a nice restaurant from an afternoon at a children's museum. "I have to change, Mommy!" she wailed between sobs. "I *have* to change! I can't go out to dinner looking like this!"

What happened? This child was taken home, of course, and allowed to change. By the time they all got to the restaurant, there was a forty-five-minute wait to get a table and it was nearly 8:30 P.M. when they all got to eat. Tired and cranky by then, the child refused to order anything but chocolate milk and plain rice with butter that had to be melted in the kitchen. She fell asleep five minutes after the food arrived, knocking her milk to the floor as she put her head down on the table.

What did the grown-ups do? You can probably guess by now. The doting dad left his dinner and took the child out to the car so she could sleep while the mom and grandmother tried unsuccessfully to enjoy the rest of their meal. After a few minutes, they gave up trying to chat and eat and had all the meals put in doggie bags to be finished later at home.

How did our friend, the child's grandmother, feel? Enchanted, she admitted sheepishly, that any child so young could have such a well-developed fashion sense. Our friend did add that she was a bit troubled at the way the child's demands were allowed to disrupt the evening completely for the adults. "But, I guess that's the way parents are raising kids today; far be it from me to judge what they do."

Face it, American parents love these prima donnas who have to look just right at all times and the princes who make moms travel 120 miles to get soccer equipment. With this much self-confidence at such an early age, today's parents believe, their kids will be CEOs of mega-million-dollar companies by the time they are twelve years old.

But their children are also becoming self-centered people who expect everybody's time, resources, and attention to be spent on their needs, first and foremost.

Let's stop right here and explain the difference between catering to a child too much (or "spoiling" the child) and attending to that child's needs for attention and love. People who cater too much place the child's needs ahead of everyone else's needs. People who attend to that child's needs for attention and love integrate periods of focused one-on-one time with the child into their lives and make the child aware of everyone's needs, not just their own. They also make the child aware that boundaries exist and are important. In learning to respect other people's boundaries, the child learns how to recognize and respect her own.

A recent "Dear Abby" column shows what happens when a self-centered child grows up. A young wife and mother asked what to do about her husband who had no desire to interact with his kids, help around the house (both he and she work full time), or share much of any time with his family. His excuse for not pitching in or participating? He needs his TV time after work and his computer time on the weekend. The wife was puzzled by his insensitivity because he was raised by doting and loving parents and other relatives and was by no means a neglected child. The reply to this wife was that maybe this man had been given so much as a child, he had no idea how to give back.

Did Abby suggest this woman teach this man how to do his part? No. She suggested the woman find other males who might be willing to interact with and act as role models to her kids on a regular basis so her kids would know what male companionship was. We agree that this solution is the best one the woman can implement, at least for now. Trying to change her husband from being the self-centered person he was brought up to be would mean trying to change years of child-centered conditioning. That approach would not be a good use of this woman's already stretched-thin energy and time. We would have also suggested the woman attend a parenting class or take assertiveness training so she could learn how to persuade her husband to change without making herself furious and driving him even further away from his family.

We asked parents, teachers, and other adults to identify characteristics that identify self-centeredness in kids. Here are their answers:

- The self-centered child is not satisfied with the family he has and does not hesitate to let his family know it. For example, he wants a family with more money. An admittedly self-centered thirteen-year-old corroborated this belief in an interview with Audrey by saying, "They should spend more money on their kids," when asked how her parents could improve their parenting. "They should not expect the kids to earn the money; they should give it to them for what they want." The self-centered child wants a family that looks better than yours does, is thinner, dresses better, and has a cooler 'do. He wants parents who stay out of his way except to do what he wants when he wants, to be respectful to his friends, and to speak only when spoken to.

- She expects parents to take her side when someone criticizes her and to blame the critic.
- He expects the school to absolve him from duties and chores and assignments he does not want to do.
- She expects her school to let her stay home, go on family vacations, and do other things besides come to school if that's what she decides she wants.
- He expects teachers to be chastened if he criticizes them for anything from their methods of teaching to their tone of voice to their expectations.
- She believes that classroom rules may apply to other students, but not to her. She interrupts when others (including the teacher) are talking; she holds lengthy one-on-one dialogues with the teachers in class whenever she wants to; she threatens to call her parents (a true reversal of rules—it used to be teachers who threatened to call the parents!) if she is displeased with a reprimand, bad grade, or any other behaviors from the teachers she doesn't like.

Why do parents cater to kids so much? A major reason is that most families have fewer kids than ever today. Families were once much larger. Having one child is becoming more common all the time. According to Carolyn White, in her "Letter from the Editor" column in *Only Child,* a quarterly publication devoted to parents of only children, "The percentage of women who have one child has more than doubled in the past 20 years up from 10% to over 23%. Only child families are the fastest growing families in this country and most industrialized Western European countries. According to the Census Bureau's Birth Expectation Survey, the number of women ages 18 to 34 in the United States who plan to have one child has increased steadily from 12.7% in 1985 to 13.9% today. In New York City over 30% of children are only children."

While having just one child allows parents to provide more of everything for that one child, it also allows overconcentration on that child. It's only natural for the child who knows he is the center of the parents' universe to believe that universe extends to the world beyond.

Another reason for catering to kids today is that it's become the custom: Parents see other parents catering to their kids. These parents become role models. Their own parents may live too far away or be seen as too old-fashioned to serve as role models. Another reason parents imitate other parents is that they want a level playing field for their children. They want their kids to have the same opportunities to shine in computer skills, sports, video games, music, and other areas, which means as many lessons and as much equipment as other kids have. We believe, however, that the main reason parents cater to kids is for the same reason anyone caters to any person—they want the kids to like them.

Does it work? For a good look at how kids really feel about indulgent parents, rent a copy of the film *Mean Girls*. Observe how Regina, the meanest girl of all, treats her mom—who tries so hard to please her in all kinds of ways that she overlooks behaviors such as Regina making out passionately with her boyfriend in her bedroom. Not only does Regina ignore her fawning mom's attempts to be friendly and gracious, but she insults her in horribly disrespectful ways, even in front of visiting friends.

Can the Six Step Plan be used to overcome self-centeredness in kids?

Yes. Kids secretly want parents who know more than they do and have their genuine best interests at heart. Here's how you can use this plan to prevent as well as cure self-centeredness in your children, starting now.

Modeling

Model fairness—including fairness to yourself. Had Jenise, the soccer mom described in the first paragraph of this chapter, been using the Six Steps, she could have said, "I'm sorry I forgot the equipment. I've got a lot on my mind with Grandma's illness (or whatever other problem is causing Mom stress). Next time, you kids make sure the equipment is in the car before we leave." Model fairness to the others in the family. The mom of a child who demands that money be spent for something she has to have can say, "This is how much money I have to spend on everyone in the family this week. This is how much has to go to the dentist, doctor, and orthodontist. There is not enough left for what your computer game costs." Model strength in the face of the child's demands. You can say, "Nagging of any kind after I have said no is unacceptable." Then, turn your attention elsewhere. Model caring for the child's well-being. "Sugar Surprise Snacks make you feel awful afterward because sugar makes you feel awful. I'm not going to buy something that makes you feel awful, even if it tastes good."

Consistency

Consistency means not giving in to the child. Once you decide how you are going to implement the other five steps in dealing with your self-centered child, you show consistency by not going back to indulging the child. The child will try six ways to Sunday to get you to change back. He will try nagging, demanding, attacking, sulking, and lots of other actions meant to wear you down. Don't give in.

......
Reinforcement

When any child is generous, sharing, shows caring, and in other ways helps others, you can say something like, "That is so generous of you to help Sally look for the cat. She needed your help, I know." Or, "I appreciate your help carrying the groceries in. I'm a bit rushed today because of all the things I have to do and your help saved me time." Acknowledge the act and tell how it helped. Eventually, the self-centered child will realize this other-centeredness is more satisfying than putting herself first all the time.

......
Showing Rational Empathy

Yes, we know—it's hard to feel empathy for self-centered kids. But you can empathize with the child's feeling that he comes first. "You know, Arden," you can say in a one-to-one talk, "you have reason to feel you are so good at twirling, you deserve private lessons and snazzy outfits. I can understand why you get mad when we spend money on other things. But your sisters need things, too. They need clothes and school supplies. We have to be fair to everyone in the family when we decide how our money will be spent."

......
Caring for Pets, Plants,
and Things in the Home

Caring for pets, plants, and other things means making sure that the self-centered child does not get more than his fair share of things and does have to share the chores of caring for the pets, plants, and things in the home. You implement this step with the self-centered child by making lists of expected chores for him and detailed step-by-step instructions for every chore. "Henry, you bathe Fuzzy. First, get the tin bucket from the garage. Then get the basket of dog shampoo and conditioner from the bathroom. Fill the bucket with warm water. . . ." Then you check up to make sure the chores were done as described. You admire the effort made—"That's great the way you got Fuzzy so clean"—then explain what didn't get done—"Now, all Fuzzy needs is to be rinsed." Then, tell how to do it: "Here's how you rinse. Turn on the hose. . . ." After a while, the self-centered child will realize you're not giving up and will participate along with everyone else. The other preparation you need to implement this step with your self-centered child is to steel yourself for his anger. He may be furious at having to give up his "most-favored child" status and pitch in like everybody else. He may refuse to cooperate, do the chores halfheartedly, and sulk openly until he sees he can't ever win. At that point, says Adlerian child psychologist Carolyn Crowder, Ph.D., this child will undoubtedly discover he likes contributing to the well-being of the household. He'll also enjoy the sense of accomplishment he gets from doing a job well.

Caring for All the People in the Family

So how do you care for your self-centered child (or children) along with all the other people in your family?

First, do some mental strengthening. Remember that indulging the self-centered behavior is not caring for anyone, especially not the self-centered child. It is teaching her that she's right to act the way she does and, at the same time, teaching other family members that they just aren't as good as she is or they'd get the same perks also. Second, implement these strategies: Ignore the self-centered child's demands— that's right, just turn a deaf ear to her as though she were a ghost who cannot communicate with you. If you do, respond to the "Mom, I'm talking to you!" by just saying, "That tone is not acceptable." Then leave her alone or turn your attention to someone else. Keep repeating the phrase "That tone is not acceptable" in a calm voice if she follows you and her demands escalate. And go someplace where you can get away from her, as quickly as possible.

Internalize this rationale: By turning away from her when her behavior is unbearable, you teach her that she is unbearable to be around. By denying her your attention, even negative attention, you are telling her that her behavior is not worth your energy at all. If she demands to know why you're ignoring her, tell her you'll answer when she changes the tone of her voice. If she does change her tone and asks you again in a nicer voice, she can be told her behavior is unpleasant. Period.

Don't say anything more. If you don't like the word *unpleasant*, you can substitute the word *unappealing*. If she thinks her behavior might be driving people away, she'll be more apt to want to change. The other children, meanwhile, will take heart by your new approach to the self-centered sibling and feel much more cared about than they did before. They'll become more able to protect themselves from her demands of them. If your spouse fails to agree with this agenda, don't despair. Your spouse may, ironically, object to your new attitude because he or she secretly thinks this self-centered child is acting out tendencies he or she was always too shy to express. No matter; *you* can model this treatment of your self-centered child with consistency, reinforcing her changes of demeanor with loving attention until she gives up her self-centered ways—at least with you. If she continues her self-centered behavior with the other children, she can be stopped. Tell all of your children, including the self-centered child, that they must treat one another with fairness and respect. Let your other children know they don't need to give in to unfair demands from anyone—not even from a sibling, no matter how much that sibling is accustomed to getting her way. Your spouse will soon tire of being the only target she has left and cooperate with your efforts to help her change.

And you know what? Unless he has a sociopathic or narcissistic personality disorder, the self-centered child knows that nobody really likes him or wants to be his friend, and he wants you to stop his behaviors. He wants you to fight him, and, deep down, he wants you to win.

If you're not sure whether your child is being self-centered or just very self-confidently assertive, take this little quiz. Mark every statement with a T if it's more true than false and F is it's more false than true.

1. She has everyone in the house walking on eggshells when she's around because everyone is afraid of saying or doing something that will make her mad.   T or F
2. He has everyone in the house walking on eggshells when he comes in a room, fearing he'll demand something that will be difficult to provide.   T or F
3. She gets huffy if she's turned down by anyone in any way.   T or F
4. He is seldom respectful to relatives or friends who visit.   T or F
5. If she says some friend or relative is "weird" and has a smirky, eyebrow-raised look of derision on her face, she expects you to stop associating with that person.   T or F
6. If he says something you serve for a meal is "weird," he does not expect to have to eat it.   T or F
7. She says negative things about you to your face a lot of the time. ("Who cut your hair? Don't tell me you went to the cheap place again. Oh, no wait, you did it yourself? God.")   T or F

Four or more T answers means the child is self-centered. Three or more T answers means he is self-centered some of the time. Two or more T answers means he is becoming self-centered. Just one T answer means he could become self-centered in no time at all. No T answers means you need to reassess your attitude toward him. You might be idealizing or idolizing him without knowing it. Have a sibling or someone else who's around him take the quiz instead.

The truth is, most children have self-centered traits that help them survive in the world. Whether these traits become uncontrollable depends on parenting of the sort that uses the Six Steps. Children who are self-centered by nature can still learn that others' needs and rights are as important as theirs.

Could it be, you may be asking at this point, that the behaviors and values encouraged in this book are relative, just embraced by our culture but maybe not other cultures? To get an idea of how, or if, parents in other cultures tend to use the Six Steps with kids, we visited with people from other cultures and asked them what child rearing is like in their countries of origin. Then we applied the Six Step model to their answers. Find out the results in chapter 16.

chapter 16

······ • ▣ • ······

Foreign and Adoptive Families

This chapter will provide "visits" with parents and children from other cultures and identify ways in which they use the Six Step Plan. This chapter will also visit with a woman who adopted five special-needs children. We know one case history is not indicative of an entire culture or the typical adoptive-parent experience. We're not trying to generalize or stereo-type. We're attempting to show you how the Six Step Plan can be applied to child rearing in different cultures and in a household of adopted children. All names have been changed, but not the people and situations.

···················
A Dutch Mom

Elsie and her husband are natives of a small town in Holland. "People in America think all of Holland is wild and crazy like Amsterdam, but believe me, it's not," Elsie said with a knowing smile. Because of Elsie's husband's job, the family has lived for years at a time in various countries and has been in the United States for five years, living in an upscale suburb of a large midwestern city. The family has two children, a boy, twelve, and a girl, eighteen, who have been raised as their parents were raised—more like children are reared in Holland than in America. Here's our view of the ways this family utilizes the Six Steps in their child rearing:

MODELING

Elsie and her husband model self-discipline and delayed gratification for their children. Elsie's children have been taught to think long and hard about what they want and to take no for an answer. "For instance," Elsie said, "our eighteen-year-old does not yet have a car. This is not strange to us. The children in Holland do not get cars until they have jobs and can afford them."

Elsie and her husband also model the keeping of boundaries with their children. "In Holland, the children go to bed at 7:00 P.M. because that's their bedtime. Then comes the adults' time when the parents are free to be together or to socialize with adult friends, without children being present."

And Elsie and her husband model acceptance and appreciation of their children as they are and avoid pressuring them to excel in sports or academics. In Holland, Elsie said, sports are peripheral activities to be pursued for enjoyment. "The children there may play a sport one or two days a week." Elsie added that parents in Holland are not concerned about making sure their kids get athletic or academic college scholarships—because they are not as insistent that their children go to college at all. "In Holland, there are three educational tracks: vocational, middle, and university," she said. The first two tracks are just as respectable and admirable for kids as the university track. She believes that what's best for the child is most important to Dutch parents.

And this family models communication and the Dutch tradition of serving home-cooked meals. "I make a real dinner every night with meat and potatoes and vegetables, and we all sit down to eat it," she said. "And we talk. We go on talking all the way through dinner and on into the evening sometimes. When we went on a camping trip recently, we would stay up late every night after dinner and just talk, talk, talk."

CONSISTENCY

As anyone familiar with the history of Holland can tell you, consistency is important to the Dutch. *No* means no in their child rearing, and rules are meant to be followed. Nagging is not tolerated—nor is whining or other behaviors meant to wear parents down.

REINFORCEMENT

Dutch parents apparently reinforce their children's desired behavior all the time in subtle ways. "We don't give a lot of praise; we don't gush," Elsie said firmly. "We just let the kids know how we think they are doing by our attitudes." Elsie said that her parents usually had a "good attitude toward me" so she always figured she was behaving in ways they wanted her to. "My parents let me know how I was doing by giving me their approval, I guess."

Dutch parents also reinforce desired behavior with support. "Our daughter studied and did well in school, by our standards," Elsie said. So when the daughter decided she would continue her post-high-school education in Holland where she has many relatives, Elsie and her husband supported the decision in every way they could.

When the children got jobs to earn money for things they needed, they were given the transportation to get to and from the jobs by Elsie. "One reason I was willing to give them rides was because we didn't think they should have cars yet."

SHOWING RATIONAL EMPATHY

The communication in this family seems to be empathic a lot of the time. In their talks at dinner, Elsie asks how the children are feeling about their activities, their friends, their teachers, and other aspects of their lives and listens with interest to their answers. The parents then offer suggestions, if any are needed, but most of all they offer empathy. When Elsie's daughter told her privately she was upset at the kinds of sexual activities going on in her high school, Elsie said she understood how shocked the daughter must be and gave her rational reasons why this daughter should not, and indeed, was not allowed to, participate in these sexual activities herself. The daughter needed this kind of rational empathic support from her mother. "She was getting a lot of pressure from her friends at school" to stop being such a prude and to participate.

CARING FOR PETS, PLANTS, AND THINGS IN THE HOME

It sounded to us as though there were no problems with this step in Elsie's home. The Dutch are known for their immaculate houses, and Elsie and her husband have carried on that tradition.

CARING FOR ALL THE PEOPLE IN THE HOME

Though Elsie's husband is away for his job much of the time, this family observes the Dutch tradition of giving the family priority. That means devoting the most attention to the children and making sure the children's needs are met. One of the main ways that Dutch parents show caring for their families is "by staying married," Elsie said. "Divorce just isn't that option for us that it is for Americans. In Holland, we know when we get married that things will sometimes be bad, but that they'll get better. We see from our parents and our other relatives that staying married is usually good."

Hispanic Daughters

Georgina and Renee work as advocates in a social service agency in the Southwest. Both are single and in their early twenties but still living in, and very much involved with, their biological families. Both their families live mainly by Mexican traditions and customs. Though Georgina was interviewed in more depth, Renee, who shares the office and was present during the interview, often concurred with what Georgina said and agreed that her family was exactly the same way. Here is the traditional Mexican family experience described by Georgina:

"You want me to count?" Georgina said when asked how many people were in her family. She then began a calculation with paper and pencil that took her about five minutes. "Thirty-six, counting my aunts and uncles and first cousins," she finally concluded. "And that's just on my mother's side." Her father's side, she said, had about twenty-nine relatives. These figures did not include the first cousins' spouses and children. Renee interrupted to say that her family had almost the exact same number of people on both sides.

Georgina said she lives with her mother and two older sisters, but is strongly connected to all of her other relatives. Here, taken from what Georgina told us about her family, are the ways that the Six Steps work in her family most of the time:

MODELING

The roles modeled are clearly defined. Parents act like parents who provide for and keep the house orderly and care for children. Older siblings model ways of succeeding in the outside world. Children act as children, playing with one another and looking up to older siblings and cousins.

CONSISTENCY

Deviations from the family codes of conduct, Georgina said, are not accepted and are dealt with by family meetings. Renee nodded in agreement.

REINFORCEMENT

The main means of reinforcing desired behaviors in Georgina's family seem to be providing a sense of belonging and acceptance. "Children get a lot of attention if they're good. They are welcomed by everyone all the time and have a lot of fun," said Georgina. "The person who causes trouble of any kind is made to feel that nobody likes him (or her). Like, for example, if you pick on someone in our family, the rest of the family makes sure you know that's wrong and ignores you." And there are tangible rewards for approved behavior. "Like cool lunch boxes," Georgina said. "If we had been good, we would get cool lunch boxes every year for school. The kind with cartoon figures." She'll never forget, she added with a blissful look, how happy and special those new lunch boxes always made her feel.

SHOWING RATIONAL EMPATHY

Georgina said she has always felt understood by members of her family—she always has someone to turn to if one relative proves unsympathetic or doesn't understand what she's feeling.

CARING FOR PETS, PLANTS, AND THINGS IN THE HOME

Georgina said that, since the age of about ten, she has been responsible for doing the dishes, keeping her part of her room clean, and caring for her dog. Before she was ten, she was being trained to do these chores by her mother. Learning how to do her share was a natural process in her house common to all females. Georgina especially loved learning to cook and now prepares meals whenever she can.

CARING FOR ALL THE PEOPLE IN THE HOME

Caring for people in Hispanic families appears to be taken very seriously. Both Georgina and Renee said their male relatives watch to make sure the female relatives are being treated properly and with respect. Other forms of caring include making sure lonely or disabled family members are visited and monitoring the children for signs that they might be "going down the wrong path," as Georgina puts it. Asked if family members socialized together, both Georgina and Renee said that their best friends are also their cousins. "We get together in groups every weekend and hang out, go to the clubs and the movies," Renee said. "We just enjoy one another's company." Any holiday is the occasion of a big barbecue or other kind of party to which a hundred or more relatives are often invited. As for care of the elderly, Georgina says one of her grandmothers complains she's lonely but always turns down numerous invitations to family parties or requests to come over and visit. "We don't know why she's like that, but she is. We never forget her, though, no matter how she acts," Georgina said. Her other grandmother "is a different story, always entertaining, always enjoying the children, always coming to the family parties. She has a ball." Both Georgina and Renee said there is no such thing in their families as elder neglect.

Both say they have friends outside their family. But, said Georgina, "they stop being outside friends. What happens is if you like these people, they become part of your family" and are given status as family members. "I now call my best friend my sister. She's as welcome in my family as I am," Georgina added.

Croatian Daughter, American Educator, Balkan Refugee Volunteer

Irina, now in her fifties, grew up in Croatia. While she has no children of her own, she has worked with many children in America as a classroom translator. She has also volunteered for many years with a Balkan refugee program, helping newcomers find apartments and jobs, get settled in schools, and adjust to American life.

MODELING

Irina's parents modeled strength in the face of difficult conditions. One of those difficult conditions was having only a small one-bedroom apartment in which to raise four boys and one girl. How did they accomplish this feat? Irina said she and her brothers slept on cots in the living room until she was a teenager. Then, she was given her own walled-off space. The parents had the bedroom.

Irina's mother modeled cheerfulness and accessibility. "She was always willing to talk to everybody about anything," Irina recalled. "People told me they couldn't talk to their own moms, but they could to mine." Her mother also modeled resourcefulness. "She did all our family washing by hand. And she also did washing for other people to help the family income. I helped her." Irina's mother was also an excellent cook and housekeeper, Irina remembered.

Irina's schoolteachers modeled firm rule following. "We stood up if a visitor came in the room, raised our hand if we needed to leave our seat for any reason, and never spoke unless spoken to." If teachers called a meeting with the parents, they expected the parents to attend. Physical activities such as sports and hiking were modeled by everyone in the community.

Other adults besides teachers and parents modeled leadership for young people by being active as scouting and physical activity leaders. Irina herself was a devoted Girl Scout for many years, and she was a high mountain climber in the Alps.

As a translator for elementary-age students in American schools, Irina found the children's classrooms very different. She was amazed that students were allowed to eat foods from machines and did not have to eat their school lunch. "It was candy and soda throughout the day. In Croatia, we always brought our lunches to school and had yogurt, homemade, at every meal." Irina was also surprised that the children here come and go in the classroom whenever they want. "There was always some child using the electric pencil sharpener, going to the restroom, getting out of their seats. The teachers would go right on teaching" no matter what the students were doing.

CONSISTENCY

Irina said that the consistency of parenting shown in Croatia allowed her and other children to survive severe financial hardships. In her volunteer work, she has seen that same consistency help Balkan families in America survive being uprooted from everything they know and be able to make new lives in America with little financial support.

The American culture seems far less consistent to Irina than the culture she grew up with. As the refugee children deal with this flexibility in rules and expectations, especially at school, they begin rebelling against their parents' attempts to impose consistency at home, Irina said. "These parents have a big challenge" in teaching the kids respect for their ways while helping them fit in to the American kids' way of life.

REINFORCEMENT

Reinforcement for children in Croatia was built into their lifestyle, Irina recalled. If they fulfilled requirements in school, they got promoted. If they ate what was served, they stayed healthy. If they finished all their food at a meal, they would not be hungry later—a good thing, because eating between meals was not allowed. And if they got their chores and homework done, they could pursue their own activities with friends. Irina believes American children are brought up differently. "American adults seem to believe that if the kids get what they want, the children will then want to do what the adults wish they would do." She believes this philosophy might work with some children—but not all.

SHOWING RATIONAL EMPATHY

Irina said that her mother's nature made her naturally empathic. "I could go to her for every problem; she always listened so well." But this step was not one that was valued all that much by others in the culture in which she grew up. From Irina's recollections, we can assume that Croatian parents were so busy dealing with survival, they didn't have time to be empathic. But the children were so busy dealing with poverty, war, fear of war, chores, and schoolwork, Irina said, they didn't seem to miss empathic relationships too much. They were just glad to have any kind of family support at all.

CARING FOR PETS, PLANTS, AND THINGS IN THE HOME

In her childhood culture, Irina said with a rueful smile, you could always tell whose parents were away working in West Germany. "Those children always had the most toys, the fanciest clothes. That's because the parents felt so guilty about not being with them, they sent them expensive gifts all the time." Her family had no room for pets and only a tiny piece of ground for planting that had to be shared with the other families in the apartment complex where they lived. "But my mom used that ground to raise red currants. We made jam from them that was so good on bread I remember it to this day," Irina said with a sigh of nostalgia. "I had few clothes, but what I had was always kept clean and ironed perfectly."

American children get many toys, Irina believes, whether their parents can afford them or not. The Balkan refugee parents find this cultural trait especially difficult. "Their kids are ashamed if they don't have as many things or if their things aren't as good as the American kids have."

CARING FOR ALL THE PEOPLE IN THE HOME

Despite lack of money, Irina's parents provided their five children with what they needed. Her mother's clothes-washing business helped make ends meet—"And this was before we had a washing machine at home." Irina said she was happy to help her mom with the washing. "And my hands show the effects to this very day!"

Funds were found for her Girl Scout and mountain-climbing activities, and the children were given what they needed to succeed in school. Two of the brothers chose a vocational education, but the other three children went "on to university," Irina said. All five are doing well financially in their adopted countries, which include New Zealand and Australia as well as the United States.

At the time of this interview, Irina was preparing to take a well-paid government position as translator of documents written in the Cyrillic alphabet.

An Adoptive Parent

As a young adult, Madelyn decided she wanted to be a mother, but she wanted children "nobody else wanted. It just seemed to be my calling." She and her husband did have one child of their own, a boy who is now married and in the process of adopting a foster child himself. Madelyn and her husband divorced amicably when their first adopted child, now thirty, was on her own and their second, now twenty-three, was a teenager. "Why did we divorce?" Madelyn thought a moment before answering the question. "I think it was because I always liked to be in charge. But my ex and I are very good friends." The twenty-three-year-old now lives with Madelyn's ex-husband. "That child had a lot of developmental disabilities, but he's doing fine now. He's also gay, which hasn't made his life any easier, I can tell you."

The three children living with Madelyn now in a cozy three-bedroom-with-den condo are Keisha, thirteen, Terence, thirteen, and Maya, eight. All are African American; all are beautiful. The girls look like models. Terence is a budding football player who could be Mr. America. Madelyn, in contrast, is a lithe, blue-eyed white woman in her late sixties who laughs easily and often.

She is with her children twenty-four hours a day because she homeschools all three. All three have learning disabilities and need individual attention, and this way, they are allowed to progress at their own pace. Madelyn is frank about her reasons for homeschooling. She said she doesn't want her children exposed to the drug culture she knows exists in public, private, and charter schools.

Here's how the Six Steps are shown in the way this mother raises her children:

MODELING

Madelyn models manners, respectful behavior, and verbal interaction. She admonished a child for unwanted behavior only once when we visited. The behavior (splashing water on all of us as we sat by the pool) was stopped. Apologies were given and accepted.

The verbal interaction in this home is carried on constantly in pleasant tones and complete sentences. Madelyn gives her full attention to the child being addressed. The children respond in kind and never whine or complain or raise their voices—at least they didn't while we were there. The youngest enjoys hugging and cuddling her mom, and Madelyn joyfully returns the affection. The other children seem to have outgrown this affectionate stage but are content to be in their mom's presence and pursue their own projects.

CONSISTENCY

Madelyn shows consistency in many ways. One of the most notable to us is not giving in to the children's immediate desires. The following statements are common examples.

When a daughter came to the kitchen while we were talking and said she was hungry, she got this response from Madelyn: "You have told me you are hungry, Maya, thank you. We'll have dinner after our guests and I finish our talk."

When her son yelled out that he wanted his mom to watch his diving into the pool, Madelyn responded, "I know you like me to watch your diving, Terence, but right now I'm busy talking to our guests."

The children never ask more than once, she said. "They just don't pester me like I know other children do their moms."

REINFORCEMENT

A lot of Madelyn's communication with her children involves reinforcement of some kind. "Thank you for bringing the towel to the pool, Keisha." "Thank you, Terence, for playing so nicely in the living room while I'm visiting with our company." "Those shoes you chose at the yard sale look so nice on your feet, Maya."

SHOWING RATIONAL EMPATHY

This step is automatic in Madelyn's child-rearing technique. "I know you want . . ." "I know you feel . . ." "You have told me you are hungry . . ." "I know we usually begin eating dinner at this time . . ." are just a few of the rational empathy statements we heard Madelyn use when explaining why something a child wanted her to do could not happen. When more stringent discipline is needed—"And of course, it is," Madelyn told us with a smile; "my kids are normal kids, after all,"—she uses consequences and a strategy she calls the sixty-second scold. "The first thirty seconds are used to let the child know how you feel about the behavior, and the second thirty seconds are used to tell the child he's too fine a person to act that way. Then you drop the matter entirely."

CARING FOR PETS, PLANTS, AND THINGS IN THE HOME

Friday is cleaning day for the whole family. They divide up the chores to be done, and everyone gets busy. They have no pets right now, but all are fond of a neighbor's poodle, always stopping to talk to it and play with it on their way to the pool. Their things are cared for carefully because there is not enough money to buy new toys if they break or get lost. They do have a TV in the home, but it's not hooked up to cable. Madelyn said she won't pay for cable, "mainly because it's so expensive, and also because so many of the cable programs and channels are just not okay. I wish those programs and channels could be blocked out and the good ones left because I know there are some excellent cable programs. But that's not possible." Not being hooked up to cable means the TV can't get local channels, either, Madelyn added. So the family uses the TV only for playing DVDs. All films brought into the home are checked out at the public library and watched *en famille*. On the day we visited, Terence was engrossed in an Erector Set project. Madelyn said he had gotten the Erector Set at a yard sale the previous day. A family project now in the planning stages is planting an herb and vegetable garden in the small backyard.

CARING FOR ALL THE PEOPLE IN THE HOME

Madelyn sees to it that the children get what they need to develop their potential. When Terence indicated a desire to "have an audience and perform" last year, Madelyn found a children's theater holding auditions for a musical. Not only was Terence chosen for a role, but the girls got parts as well. Madelyn and the children visit museums and the zoo every weekend, and they see friends they have made in the home-schooling network Madelyn found.

She takes the children traveling every summer to visit their siblings—Madelyn's other children—who are living away from home. They also visit other relatives, stopping to enjoy historical or scenic sites of interest and camping out at night, "except for those times when we Motel 6 it to take showers and get cleaned up."

The whole family goes to church every Sunday, and the children are involved in youth activities there. "Faith is very important to us all," Madelyn said. In fact, she added serenely, "It's my faith in God, my Higher Power, that keeps me going. I couldn't do all this without it."

Well, you are probably saying now, this is all lovely, but what happens later on? How will the children react when they are exposed to the outside world and the not-so-nice people in it? How will they continue their education if they have never been to "real" school? These questions are legitimate. But the anxiety inherent in them is unfounded. These children will do just fine, we believe, because every one of them is developing such a strong sense of self. They know who they are, how valued they are, and how to make people like them; they want to interact with others as teachers, as friends, and in other helper roles. They know what their values are, and they know how to take care of themselves and their home. All these "teachings" now internalized by these kids augur well for their happiness and success in their adult lives.

Index

····· ◘ ······

About the Authors

Audrey Ricker, Ph.D., has written four books for major publishers. She coauthored two parenting books, including the *New York Times* best seller *Backtalk: Four Steps to Ending Rude Behavior in Your Kids* and *Whining: Three Steps to Stopping It Before the Tears and Tantrums Start.* She has also published a book on nutrition, *Smart Guide to Vitamins and Healing Supplements,* and a book combining her interests in parenting and nutrition entitled *Bad Attitude: Reverse Your Child's Rudeness in One Week—with Food.* Dr. Ricker received her doctorate in education from the University of Arizona with an emphasis in media literacy. She lives in Tucson and has one son and two granddaughters.

Robert E. Calmes, Ed.D., is a licensed psychologist and Professor Emeritus of Education at the University of Arizona, where he has taught for more than thirty years. He has published more than 115 articles in academic journals and has written six books, including *Positive Experiences in Our Children's Morality and Valuing: What Parents and Others Can Do.* He is the Dean of Anger Management for the Adult Rehabilitation Program of the Tucson Salvation Army.

Lynn Wiese Sneyd is the author of *Holistic Parenting: Raising Children to a New Physical, Emotional, and Spiritual Well-Being.* She has been published in *Fitness Plus, Tucson Monthly,* the *Arizona Daily Star,* and the *Milwaukee Journal Sentinel.* Ms. Wiese Sneyd has worked as the community relations manager for Barnes & Noble and as director of public relations for the Russell Public Affairs Group. She lives in Tucson with her husband and two daughters.

The authors love to communicate with parents and others involved in creating a home and family. Readers who have questions and comments on any part of this book are invited to visit www.happyfamilieshappen.com.